# The Art of the
# HAMBURGER

# The Art of the
# HAMBURGER

CHARTWELL
BOOKS, INC.

## Credits

**Commissioning Editor:** Will Steeds

**Project Editor:** Lisa Dyer

**Consultant:** Richard J. S. Gutman

**Design:** Lindsey Johns at The Design Revolution, Brighton, England

**Illustration:** Chrissie Sloan

**Food photography:** Amanda Heywood

**Artifact photography:** Louis Fliger, Larry Kantor, Craig Kohlruss, Neal Lauron, Mark Robertson

**Production:** Neil Randles, Karen Staff

**Color reproduction:** HBM Print Pte., Ltd., Singapore

**Printed in Spain**

CHARTWELL BOOKS

A division of Book Sales, Inc.

114 Northfield Avenue

Edison, N.J. 08837, USA

CLB 4897

This edition published 1996 by CLB International

©1996 CLB International, Godalming, Surrey, England

ISBN 0-7858-0704-7

### Acknowledgments

The Publishers particularly wish to thank Richard J. S. Gutman, Harry Sperl and Leora Kahn for their advice and help throughout the project.

Full acknowledgments are given on page 93, together with the picture credits.

### Publisher's note

The memorabilia and artifacts featured in this title are for illustration purposes only; none of the restaurants or organisations whose artifacts are featured have been involved in any way in creating the recipes that appear in this book, and the Publishers wish to state that the use of particular artifacts with specific recipes is in no way intended to imply that the recipe in question has been supplied, created or approved by the particular restaurant or organisation.

# contents

# HAMBURGER HISTORY

**It's hard to beat a hamburger. It is easy to make, easy to eat, and the perfect food to complement with add-ons, from simple ketchup, through lettuce, tomato, and onion, and right on up to pineapple and avocado. The sky's the limit when it comes to the ingredients you can pile on your hamburger.**

"Buy a bagfull!" was a slogan of the White Tower chain in the 1920s, when one dollar would get you twenty mini hamburgers – even if they were only an ounce in weight, sandwiched into a tiny bun. These little novelties were a big hit in an era when Americans went crazy for the burger, and the rest of the world was soon to catch on.

The hamburger's introduction to the North American palate is the subject of controversy. Although the hamburg steak appeared on New York's Delmonico's Restaurant menu as early as 1834, it wasn't until the beef was sandwiched between bread slices that the hamburger was born. Some advocate that German immigrants from Hamburg first served up the delicacy at the St.

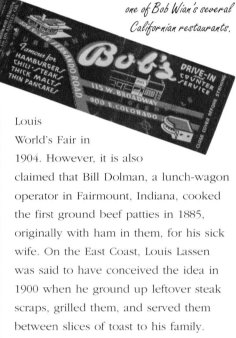

BELOW: *A 1948 matchbook advertising one of Bob Wian's several Californian restaurants.*

Louis World's Fair in 1904. However, it is also claimed that Bill Dolman, a lunch-wagon operator in Fairmount, Indiana, cooked the first ground beef patties in 1885, originally with ham in them, for his sick wife. On the East Coast, Louis Lassen was said to have conceived the idea in 1900 when he ground up leftover steak scraps, grilled them, and served them between slices of toast to his family.

Regardless of who invented it, the hamburger became a phenomenon, with each purveyor serving it his own way. At Cornell University, in Ithaca, New York, John Love dished out "desdemonas" from his horse-drawn wagon around World War I. This was ground beef, mixed with an egg, and fried.

LEFT: *A 1930s postcard of the Owl Night Lunch wagon, Dearborn, Michigan.*

Once the exclusive offering of itinerant vendors, hamburgers soon became the staple of new chain-food operations. The early fast-food business, dominated by White Castle and their competitor, White Tower, were built on the hamburger. Their little, gleaming white buildings were distinctive and eye-catching, and they lent a new air of respectability to the burger, which previously had only been sold in sometimes seedy hamburger "joints."

The proliferation of hamburger restaurants, diners, soda fountains, and lunch counters all contributed to the growing popularity of hamburgers. Not only was the working class grabbing a quick bite, but America was on the move, and travelers were stopping along the roadside for meals.

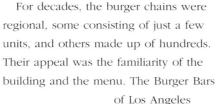

ABOVE: *The McDonald's in Allentown, Pennsylvania, in 1972, with its classic golden arches.*

For decades, the burger chains were regional, some consisting of just a few units, and others made up of hundreds. Their appeal was the familiarity of the building and the menu. The Burger Bars of Los Angeles were recognizable by the neon "Yum Yum" glowing over the door, and the hamburger would be the same, whether bought in Reseda or Canoga Park.

By the 1960s, the fast-food industry had truly arrived. When McDonald's first advertised nationally in *Life* magazine on October 5, 1962, they were well on their way to transforming and standardizing the hamburger business.

ABOVE: *An early appearance of the famed J. Wellington Wimpy — self-confessed burger addict of the '30s.*

Today, any restaurant in the world that advertises American food will offer a hamburger on its menu. It may be a more elaborate version of the simple "burger on a bun," or it may be only a basic burger, but its popularity remains undiminished. In the Washington, D.C., chain of six Silver Diners, the menu includes dozens of choices of Blue Plate Specials, healthy foods, sandwiches, and salads. But the hamburger is ordered more often than anything else.

**by Richard J.S. Gutman**

ABOVE: *A selection of matchbooks, produced to advertise competing restaurants in a fierce market.*

# BURGER BASICS

Burgers are supposed to be a quick and easy food to prepare, as well as a tasty and enjoyable culinary experience, but there are a few tricks to insure successful burger making and cooking. Carefully read the ingredients and the cooking method before you start, preparing all the necessary ingredients. All the burgers in this book serve four, and all the accompaniments are enough for four, plus some left over. Remember to leave some time to let the burgers "rest" before cooking, if possible, because this helps them keep their shape. Also consider the time it will take you to prepare an outdoor grill, if you are cooking by this method.

## CHOOSING THE MEAT

Burgers require a relatively short cooking time, so tender cuts are generally chosen for grinding. Beef is probably the most common choice for burgers, but lamb, pork, veal, turkey, chicken, and fish can all be used successfully. Ground chuck steak makes the juiciest burgers, and ground round steak is another good choice. Sirloin can be used, but needs a little extra moistening. Most supermarkets sell ground meats and list the fat contents; 80% lean is considered fatty, 85% lean moderately fatty, and 90% lean is very lean. If you prefer to use very lean meat, add a little liquid to the meat mixture to help keep the burgers moist during cooking. Two tablespoons of stock, water, milk, cream, sour cream, or even a handful of crushed ice for each pound of meat can be added to help keep burgers moist and self-basting.

If you cannot find the ground meat you want at your local supermarket, you can ask your butcher to grind the meat to order for you. You can also grind your own meat at home with an old-fashioned meat grinder or a food processor that is fitted with the metal

HAMBURGER
ON A ROLL
"Buy 'em by the bag"

blade. Most of the recipes in the book suggest using a food processor, but be very careful not to overprocess the meat. Using the pulse button will give you a little more control and help avoid a solid consistency. If the food processor is a small one, or the meat quantity is large, work in two or more batches so the meat does not become mushy.

Most of the burger recipes on the following pages are flexible and easy to adapt. If you like the sound of a lamb recipe, but don't like lamb, substitute beef, veal, or a mixture of the two. If you like spicy food, add extra chili or hot pepper sauce, or if you want your burgers less spicy, omit the chili.

## SHAPING THE BURGERS

A burger should be firm, but not compact. Combine the ingredients as lightly as possible; they should be completely mixed, but the burgers should not be dense. Using your hands is the best way, but a fork works well, too. To shape the patties, first dampen your hands with cold water. This prevents the mixture from becoming sticky because the water repels any fats in the mixture.

## COOKING BURGERS

Burgers can be barbecued outdoors on a grill, indoors under a broiler, pan-fried, or even oven-baked. Outdoor charcoal barbecuing gives a wonderful flavor, but isn't always practical or possible. However, if barbecuing, remember to let the charcoal burn until it is covered with white ash. The center will be the hottest point with the outside edges cooler. Always grease the grill rack with oil, using a barbecuing brush or a thick wad of paper towels dipped in oil. Start cooking burgers in the center to sear them, then move them over to an outside edge to a slightly lower temperature to complete the cooking. Gas or electric grills can be adjusted more easily.

If using an oven broiler, place the oven rack 4–6 inches from the heat. Always preheat the broiler. Line a broiler pan with foil and grease it very lightly; this makes cleaning up much easier. Black ridged grill pans, also called stove-top broilers, make a great substitute for grills and broilers. They need to be preheated first over a medium–high heat, then brushed with oil before cooking begins.

ABOVE: This sign for Angelo's, in Anaheim, California, dates from 1965.

Refrigerate the burgers before cooking, if possible for 1–2 hours. Most burgers benefit from several hours resting, because it lets the meat relax and the flavors develop, and helps the burgers keep their shape during cooking. Beef burgers are the exception, because they begin to oxidize and lose color within a few hours. Burgers are best made fresh. They do not really freeze well because the water content affects the cooking, and since they are so quick to make, it is not really necessary.

Burgers are equally delicious when pan-fried. A large, heavy-based skillet is ideal, and 2 tablespoons of any vegetable oil is usually enough for four burgers. A nonstick skillet can be brushed with a minimum amount of oil. Sometimes more delicate burgers, such as those made with fish, can be started in a pan for crispness, then finished off in a medium–hot oven to cook through. Although beef, lamb, and veal can be eaten rare, pork, chicken, and turkey burgers should be well cooked throughout. To test if the burger is done, press it in the center. If the meat feels firm and springs back, it is ready to eat; if it feels soft, it is still rare. If in doubt, cut into the center of one burger just to check that the juices are running clear. Although cooking times will vary somewhat, the chart below is a useful general guide.

| Rare | 6–8 minutes, turning once |
| Medium-rare | 8–10 minutes, turning once |
| Well done | 10–12 minutes, turning once |

HUHN'S DRIVE-IN and SODA LOUNGE
BELMAR, N. J.

# NEW ENGLAND & THE MID-ATLANTIC STATES

# Pilgrim Turkey Burgers
## with Cranberry-Citrus Relish

*This recipe celebrates the flavors of a traditional Thanksgiving dinner. The relish must be prepared the day before.*

1¹/₂ pounds ground
turkey
2 scallions, finely
chopped
1 stalk celery, finely
chopped
1 clove garlic, crushed
1 tablespoon heavy cream

Salt and freshly ground
black pepper
2–3 tablespoons
vegetable oil
Red oak leaf lettuce
4 rye or whole-wheat bread
slices, toasted

### Cranberry-Citrus Relish

2 cups cranberries,
fresh or thawed if frozen
1 small orange, quartered
and deseeded
1 small lemon, quartered and
deseeded

1 small lime, cut into small
pieces and deseeded
¹/₂ cup sugar, or to taste

1. Prepare the relish. Put the cranberries, orange, lemon, and lime in the bowl of a food processor and process until finely chopped. Do not overprocess or the relish will be too slushy. Transfer to a bowl and stir in the sugar. Cover and refrigerate overnight. Add more sugar to taste before serving, if necessary.

2. Put the ground turkey in a bowl and add the scallions, celery, garlic, and cream. Season with salt and pepper. Using a fork, toss the ingredients until well combined. Shape into 4 patties and refrigerate for 20 minutes.

3. Heat the oil in a large heavy-based skillet over a medium heat. Add the patties and cook for 6–8 minutes, turning once, until crisp and golden.

4. Arrange a few lettuce leaves on each slice of toasted bread. Place a burger on each, top each burger with a spoonful of the Cranberry–Citrus Relish, and serve immediately.

*RIGHT: Kelly's restaurant, Rhode Island – a classic '60s sign devised to attract the attention of passing motorists.*

# Pennsylvania Dutch Ham Burgers
## with Pineapple and Homemade Coleslaw

*If you prefer, substitute a spoonful of your favorite chutney for the pineapple, and use apple juice instead of pineapple to glaze the ham.*

4 ham steaks, about
   1/2 inch thick

4 slices canned pineapple in
   its own juice, with the
   juice reserved

2 tablespoons brown
   sugar

1/2-inch piece fresh
   ginger, grated

1 tablespoon lemon juice

1 tablespoon powdered
   mustard

4 flat poppyseed bread rolls,
   sliced and toasted

### Homemade Coleslaw

4 tablespoons mayonnaise

2 tablespoons cider or white
   wine vinegar

2 tablespoons milk

1 teaspoon sugar

Salt and freshly ground
   white pepper

1/2 small white
   cabbage, finely
   shredded

2 carrots, grated
   or shredded

3 scallions,
   finely sliced

1. Prepare the coleslaw. Put the mayonnaise, vinegar, milk, and sugar in a large bowl. Season with salt and pepper and beat until smooth. Add the cabbage, carrots, and scallions, tossing to coat well. Cover and refrigerate until ready to serve.

2. Put 1/2 cup of the reserved pineapple juice in a small saucepan. Add the brown sugar, ginger, lemon juice, and powdered mustard. Bring the mixture to a boil over a medium heat, then simmer for 3–4 minutes until it has thickened to make a glaze.

3. Preheat a broiler. Snip the edges of the ham steaks and arrange them on a greased foil-lined broiler pan. Spoon a little glaze over each steak and broil for 4–5 minutes, without turning and basting after about 2 minutes. About 1 minute before the end of the cooking time, top the ham with the pineapple slices.

4. Arrange the ham steaks on the toasted roll bottoms and drizzle over any pan juices. Spoon a little coleslaw over each, cover with the roll tops, and serve immediately with any extra coleslaw.

# Red Flannel Hashburgers

*Red beets and corned beef are a traditional New England combination.*

6 slices bacon, diced

1 onion, chopped

2 medium-large potatoes, cooked and diced

12 ounces corned beef, chopped

3 medium beets, cooked and diced

4 tablespoons heavy cream

2 tablespoons chopped fresh parsley

Salt and freshly ground black pepper

1 egg, lightly beaten

3–4 tablespoons vegetable oil

4 slices rye bread, lightly toasted

Fresh parsley sprigs, to garnish (optional)

Green salad, to serve

1. Put the bacon in a medium-size skillet and place over a medium heat. When the bacon fat begins to melt, cook for 3–5 minutes, stirring occasionally, until the bacon is crisp and golden. Remove the bacon slices from the skillet and drain on several layers of paper towels.

2. Add the onion to the remaining fat in the skillet and cook for 2–3 minutes, until softened and just beginning to color. Transfer to a mixing bowl, reserving any extra bacon drippings that are left over.

3. Add the bacon, potatoes, corned beef, beets, cream, and parsley to the bowl. Season with salt and pepper, and mix well. Add the beaten egg and mix well to blend. Heat any reserved bacon fat and the vegetable oil in a clean skillet over a medium heat. Spoon the mixture into the skillet in 4 mounds and, using a large spoon, shape the mounds into patties. The mixture will not stick together, but will cook into a rounded shape. Press each patty to flatten it slightly and cook over a medium–low heat for 3–5 minutes until the bottoms of the burgers are browned.

4. Carefully turn each patty over and continue cooking for about 5 minutes more, until golden, adding a little more oil to the skillet if necessary. Top each toast slice with a burger, garnish with parsley, if using, and serve immediately with the green salad.

only the best steers may enter

HAMBURG HEAVEN

# Maple-Barbecued Pork Burgers
## with Baked Beans

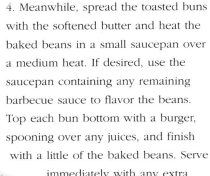

*Use real maple syrup to flavor the barbecue sauce; imitation maple syrup will not give the authentic flavor.*

1¹/2 pounds ground pork

1 teaspoon powdered mustard

2–3 dashes hot pepper sauce

Salt and pepper

4 burger buns, split and toasted

2 tablespoons butter, softened

Baked beans, to serve

### Maple-Barbecue Sauce

1 tablespoon vegetable oil

1/2 small onion, finely chopped

1/2 cup Easy Barbecue Sauce, see page 89, or a good-quality commercial variety

1/2 cup real maple syrup

1 tablespoon cider or white wine vinegar

1 teaspoon dark brown sugar

Hot pepper sauce (optional)

1. Prepare the barbecue sauce. Heat the vegetable oil in a saucepan over a medium heat. Add the onions and cook for 2–3 minutes, until softened. Stir in the barbecue sauce, maple syrup, vinegar, brown sugar, and a few dashes of hot pepper sauce, if using. Simmer for about 2 minutes, stirring frequently, until the flavors blend. Set aside and let cool.

2. Put the ground pork in a bowl and sprinkle over the powdered mustard and hot pepper sauce. Season with salt and pepper. Using a fork, toss the ingredients to combine well. Drizzle over 1–2 tablespoons of the barbecue sauce and toss gently to blend. Shape the mixture into 4 patties and refrigerate for 20 minutes.

3. Preheat a broiler. Arrange the patties on a greased foil-lined broiler pan. Spoon a little barbecue sauce on each patty and grill for 6–8 minutes, turning once and basting with more barbecue sauce every 2–3 minutes.

4. Meanwhile, spread the toasted buns with the softened butter and heat the baked beans in a small saucepan over a medium heat. If desired, use the saucepan containing any remaining barbecue sauce to flavor the beans. Top each bun bottom with a burger, spooning over any juices, and finish with a little of the baked beans. Serve immediately with any extra beans.

# Toronto Turkey Burgers
## *with Canadian Wild Rice*

*Wild rice gives these burgers a crunchy, nutty texture, in addition to an attractive dark fleck of color.*

1 teaspoon salt

1/3 cup wild rice

1 pound 2 ounces diced turkey breast

2 scallions, chopped

1 clove garlic, crushed

1/2 teaspoon dried thyme

1-2 tablespoons fresh breadcrumbs

1 tablespoon heavy cream

Dash Worchestershire sauce

Salt and freshly ground black pepper

2-3 tablespoons vegetable oil

4 slices white bread, toasted

Fresh thyme sprigs, to garnish

### Sautéed Onions and Mushrooms

2-3 tablespoons vegetable oil

2 large onions, sliced

2 cups sliced mushrooms

1/2 teaspoon thyme

1-2 tablespoons water or vegetable stock

Dash soy sauce

1. Bring a large saucepan of water to a boil. Add the salt and wild rice. Simmer for about 45 minutes, until the rice is very tender. Drain well and set aside to cool.

2. Prepare the onions and mushrooms. Pour the vegetable oil into a large skillet and heat over a medium heat. Add the onions and cook for 5–7 minutes, stirring occasionally, until softened and lightly colored. Add the mushrooms, thyme, water or stock, and soy sauce, and cook for 5 minutes more, until the vegetables are softened and well browned. Transfer to an ovenproof dish and keep warm in a moderate oven.

3. Put the turkey into the bowl of a food processor and chop coarsely. Transfer to a bowl and add the wild rice, scallions, garlic, thyme, 1 tablespoon of the breadcrumbs, cream, Worchestershire sauce, and seasoning. Toss with a fork to mix. Add the remaining breadcrumbs, if necessary, and shape into 4 patties.

4. Heat the oil in a large skillet over a medium–high heat and cook the patties for 5–7 minutes, turning once, until golden. Arrange some of the onions and mushrooms on each of the toast slices and top each with a burger. Garnish with more of the vegetables and the thyme sprigs, and serve immediately.

# Maine Lobster Burgers
## with Chili-Chive Mayonnaise

*These delicious burgers are extravagant, but well worth the extra expense for a special occasion. Use frozen rock lobster tails because they are easy to remove from the shell.*

2 tablespoons vegetable oil

1 small onion, finely chopped

1 stalk celery, finely chopped

1/2 red or yellow bell pepper, finely chopped

1 small clove garlic, crushed

1 tablespoon sweet chili sauce

2 tablespoons chopped fresh chives

1 tablespoon chopped fresh parsley

Juice of 1/2 lemon

1 pound 9 ounces lobster tail meat (about 3 8-ounce tails)

4 slices challah bread, toasted

### Chili-Chive Mayonnaise

6 tablespoons mayonnaise

2 tablespoons chopped fresh chives

1 tablespoon sweet chili sauce, or to taste

Lemon juice, to taste

2 tablespoons milk

1. Prepare the mayonnaise. In a small bowl, stir together the mayonnaise, chives and chilli sauce. Add a little lemon juice to taste. Stir in the milk to thin the mixture slightly, then cover the prepared mayonnaise and refrigerate until ready to serve.

2. Heat the oil in a medium-size skillet over a medium–high heat. Add the onion, celery, bell pepper, and garlic. Cook for 2–3 minutes, until the vegetables are softened and fragrant. Stir in the chili sauce, chives, parsley, and lemon juice. Transfer to a plate and refrigerate to cool the mixture quickly.

3. Using kitchen scissors, cut along the center length of the thin undershell of the lobster tails, then trim away the shell completely. Pull the meat out of the shells and cut into chunks. Put the meat in the bowl of a food processor and process until coarsely chopped. Transfer to a bowl.

4. Add the cooled vegetable mixture to the lobster meat and shape into 4 oval-shaped patties. Preheat a broiler. Arrange the patties on a greased foil-lined broiler pan and broil close to the heat for 3–4 minutes (it will not be necessary to turn them). Place on the toasted bread, top each with a little of the Chili–Chive Mayonnaise, and serve immediately with any extra mayonnaise.

# Clamburgers
## with Tartar Sauce

*These burgers will remind you of the tasty*
*seafood bought on the beach front or by the wharf.*
*There is no need to add any salt to the recipe.*

2 x 7.5-ounce cans clams, drained well

4 slices bacon, diced

5–6 tablespoons vegetable oil

1 small onion, finely chopped

1 stalk celery, finely chopped

1¹/₂ cups coarsely chopped mushrooms

2 tablespoons finely chopped fresh parsley

1 cup fresh white breadcrumbs

1 egg, lightly beaten

Freshly ground black pepper

Lettuce leaves

Cherry tomatoes and sliced scallions, to garnish

Tartar Sauce, see page 87, to serve

1. Chop the clams coarsely and set aside. Put the bacon in a cold skillet and place over medium heat. When the bacon fat begins to melt, stir the pieces and cook for 3–5 minutes until the bacon is crisp and golden. Remove and drain on paper towels.

2. Add 2 tablespoons of oil to the remaining fat in the skillet and stir in the onion and celery. Cook for about 2 minutes, stirring occasionally, until the vegetables are softened. Add the mushrooms and cook for 3–4 minutes more, until they are golden. Stir in the chopped clams, fresh parsley, and breadcrumbs until well blended. Remove the mixture from the heat and let cool.

3. When cool, stir in the beaten egg and season with pepper. Shape into 4 patties and refrigerate for at least 1 hour.

4. Heat 3–4 tablespoons of oil in a skillet until very hot, but not smoking. Add the patties and cook for 3–4 minutes, turning once, until golden. Remove and drain on paper towels. Arrange lettuce leaves on 4 plates and top each serving with a burger. Garnish with cherry tomatoes and scallions, and serve immediately with the Tartar Sauce.

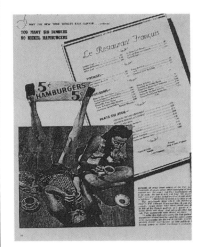

*ABOVE: A December, 1939, magazine article speculated that the New York World's Fair flopped because there were "No nickel hamburgers."*

# Nova Scotia Salmon Burgers
## with Cucumber Salad and Dill-Caper Mayonnaise

*These delicious "burgers" have a distinct Canadian influence and use one of its best known products — fine Atlantic salmon.*

1¹/₂ pounds fresh salmon fillet, cut into 12 small pieces

2 tablespoons lemon juice

¹/₂ teaspoon cracked black pepper

About 2 tablespoons vegetable oil

Lettuce leaves

4 slices sourdough bread, toasted

Fresh dill sprigs, to garnish

### Cucumber Salad

2 medium cucumbers, peeled and thinly sliced

¹/₄ cup white wine vinegar

1–2 tablespoons sugar

1 tablespoon chopped fresh dill

Salt and freshly ground black pepper

### Dill-Caper Mayonnaise

4 tablespoons mayonnaise

2 tablespoons chopped fresh dill

1–2 teaspoons Pernod, or other anise-flavor liqueur

1–2 teaspoons capers, rinsed, drained, and chopped

Salt and freshly ground black pepper

1. Prepare the cucumbers. Put the cucumbers in a medium-size bowl with the vinegar, sugar, and dill. Season with salt and pepper, and toss well to combine. For best results, let stand for at least 2 hours, stirring occasionally, until the cucumbers soften slightly.

2. Prepare the mayonnaise. Put the mayonnaise, dill, Pernod, and capers in a small bowl. Season with salt and pepper, and beat until blended. Cover and refrigerate until ready to serve.

3. About 30 minutes before serving, put the salmon in a shallow glass dish. Sprinkle with the lemon juice, black pepper, and 1–2 teaspoons vegetable oil. Turn the salmon to coat well and leave to marinate for 20 minutes.

4. Heat 1 tablespoon of oil in a large nonstick skillet over a high heat. Drain the salmon and add to the pan. Cook the salmon pieces for about 1 minute on each side, or longer if very thick, then cover the skillet and remove it from the heat. Let stand for 2–3 minutes, so the fish can continue cooking while remaining moist.

5. Brush the sourdough toast with a little oil, if you like, and arrange the lettuce leaves on top. Drain some of the Cucumber Salad and arrange on the lettuce. Top each serving with 3 salmon pieces and a spoonful of the prepared mayonnaise. Garnish with dill and serve the burgers immediately with any remaining salad.

*BELOW: Ceramic, burger-shaped salt, pepper, and mustard holders, dating from the '70s.*

# Southern-Fried Chicken Burgers
## with Hot Pepper Mayonnaise and Corn Salsa

*The buttermilk in the recipe tenderizes the chicken and accentuates the Southern flavors.*

| | |
|---|---|
| 1¹/2 pounds boneless, skinless chicken breast, cut into small pieces | 1 teaspoon salt |
| 1 egg white | Freshly ground black pepper |
| 3 tablespoons buttermilk | 1/2 cup dry breadcrumbs |
| 1/2 small onion, finely chopped | 1 cup cornmeal |
| | 4–6 tablespoons vegetable oil |

### Hot Pepper Mayonnaise

| | |
|---|---|
| 3 tablespoons mayonnaise | 1/4 teaspoon hot pepper sauce, or to taste |
| 1 tablespoon buttermilk | |

### Corn Salsa

| | |
|---|---|
| 14-ounce can corn kernels | Juice of 1 lime |
| 1 small fresh red or green chili, deseeded and finely chopped | 1 tablespoon corn oil |
| | 1 teaspoon sugar |
| 1 red bell pepper, finely chopped | 1 tablespoon chopped fresh cilantro |
| | Salt |

1. Prepare the salsa. Combine the corn kernels, chili, red bell pepper, lime juice, oil, sugar, cilantro, and salt to taste in a mixing bowl. Cover and let stand for about 1 hour before serving so the flavors can develop.

2. Prepare the mayonnaise. In a small bowl, mix together the mayonnaise, hot pepper sauce, and buttermilk. Cover and refrigerate until ready to serve.

3. Put the chicken pieces in the bowl of a food processor and process until coarsely chopped.

4. In a medium mixing bowl, beat the egg white until foamy. Beat in the buttermilk, onion, salt, pepper, and breadcrumbs. Add the chopped chicken. Using a fork, toss lightly to combine. Add a little more breadcrumbs if the mixture seems too wet. Shape the mixture into 4 patties.

5. Put the cornmeal in a shallow dish or plate and dip the patties in, one at a time, to coat on all sides. Transfer to a plate, cover, and refrigerate for about 30 minutes.

6. Preheat the oven to 350°F. Heat 2 tablespoons of the vegetable oil in a heavy-based, preferably nonstick, skillet over a medium–high heat until very hot, but not smoking. Add the patties to the pan and cook for about 1 minute on each side until just golden. Transfer the burgers to a greased, foil-lined baking sheet and bake for 10–12 minutes, until cooked through. Transfer to serving plates, top with the mayonnaise, and serve with the salsa.

# Georgia Chicken Burgers
## *with Peanut–Cucumber Relish*

*This "burger" is really a chicken fillet cooked whole, but served like a burger.*

2 tablespoons vegetable oil

4 boneless, skinless chicken breasts, about 6 ounces each

4 tablespoons Dijon mustard

Salt and freshly ground black pepper

1 cucumber, scored and thinly sliced

### Marbled Mustard Mayonnaise

3–4 tablespoons mayonnaise

2 tablespoons Dijon mustard

Fresh parsley sprigs, to garnish

### Peanut-Cucumber Relish

1¼ cups shelled, unsalted peanuts

1 large cucumber, scored, deseeded, and diced

2–3 scallions, finely chopped

1 clove garlic, crushed

3–4 tablespoons peanut or vegetable oil

2 tablespoons cider vinegar

1 tablespoon chopped fresh parsley

Salt

Cayenne pepper

1. Prepare the relish. Spread the peanuts in a single layer on a baking sheet and toast under a preheated hot broiler until lightly golden. In a bowl, combine the peanuts, cucumber, scallions, garlic, oil, vinegar, parsley, and salt and cayenne pepper to taste. Cover and let stand for about 1 hour before serving.

2. Prepare the mayonnaise. Put the mayonnaise in a small bowl and gently swirl in the mustard, but do not blend completely. Cover and refrigerate until ready to serve.

3. Heat 2 tablespoons of oil in a heavy-based skillet and place over a medium–high heat. Alternatively, oil a black, ridged grill pan. Rub each chicken breast with a little oil, then rub each with one-quarter of the mustard. Season the chicken with salt and pepper.

4. When the skillet or pan is just beginning to smoke, add the chicken breasts and cook for about 3 minutes on each side, until slightly charred and cooked. Arrange the cucumber slices in four rounds,

slightly larger than the burgers. Top each round with a burger and spoon on a little of the Marbled Mustard Mayonnaise. Garnish with parsley and serve immediately with the Peanut–Cucumber Relish.

# The Elvis Burger

*Apparently Elvis adored fried banana and peanut butter sandwiches, which Graceland's kitchen was prepared to make at all hours of the day. The Elvis Burger was inspired by this famous sandwich.*

**8 slices white bread, toasted**

**8 tablespoons peanut butter**

**1 large banana, thinly sliced**

**3 tablespoons vegetable oil**

**2 tablespoons butter**

**8 slices bacon, thinly sliced crosswise**

**Lettuce leaves**

**Hamburger corn relish**

1. Place the bread slices on a work counter. Using a 3 1/2–4 inch round cookie cutter, cut out 8 rounds. Discard the crusts. Spread 4 of the slices evenly with the peanut butter and cover each with a thin, even layer of sliced banana.

2. Heat 1 tablespoon of the vegetable oil in a large heavy-based skillet over a medium–high heat and fry the bacon for 3–4 minutes, until crisp. Remove from the skillet and drain on paper towels. Reserve the oil in the skillet. Divide the crisp bacon among the layered bread slices.

Top with the remaining bread slices, pressing the top against the filling to seal.

3. Return the skillet to a medium–high heat, and add the remaining oil and butter. Carefully add the sandwich "burgers" and fry for 2–3 minutes until golden, turning once. Remove and drain on paper towels.

4. Line 4 plates with lettuce leaves and top each with a "burger" and a spoonful of corn relish. Serve immediately.

*ABOVE: Fast food and rock 'n roll — a classic combination!*

# Spicy Pork Po' Boy Burgers

## *with Creole Sauce*

*The po'boy, or poorboy, is an enormous submarine sandwich made with sliced meats and lots of toppings. This burger-style po'boy is topped with a spicy Creole Sauce.*

| | |
|---|---|
| 1 pork tenderloin, about 1 pound 2 ounces | French-style baguette, cut into 4 x 5-inch sections |
| 3–4 tablespoons vegetable oil | Lettuce leaves |
| 2 tablespoons cider vinegar | 2 medium tomatoes, sliced |
| 1–2 cloves garlic, crushed | 1 onion, thinly sliced |
| 1/4 teaspoon crushed hot peppers, or to taste | |

### Creole Sauce

| | |
|---|---|
| 2 tablespoons vegetable oil | 1 small fresh green chili, deseeded and chopped |
| 1 teaspoon hot paprika | 1 teaspoon brown sugar |
| 1 small onion, finely chopped | 1/2 teaspoon dried thyme |
| 2 stalks celery, finely chopped | 14-ounce can chopped tomatoes |
| 1 small green or red bell pepper, finely chopped | 1–2 tablespoons chopped parsley |
| 1 clove garlic, crushed | Salt |

1. Prepare the sauce. Heat the oil in a large skillet over a medium–high heat. Stir in the paprika, onion, celery, bell pepper, garlic, and chili. Cook for 2 minutes, until beginning to brown.

2. Add the brown sugar, thyme, and tomatoes, and reduce the heat to medium–low. Cook for about 20 minutes, stirring occasionally, until the sauce thickens and the tomato liquid is evaporated. Stir in the parsley and season with salt. Transfer to a bowl and set aside until ready to serve.

3. Prepare the burgers. Place the pork on a cutting board. Holding a knife at a 45° angle, slice the pork into 8 thin scallops. Arrange in a shallow dish, and add 2–3 tablespoons of the oil, the vinegar, garlic, and crushed hot peppers. Turn the scallops to coat well. Set aside for 30 minutes to marinate, then drain.

4. Heat a ridged, black grill pan over a medium–high heat and brush with a little of the remaining oil. Add the marinated scallops and cook for 2–3 minutes, turning once, until browned and just cooked through. Remove from the pan and drain on paper towels.

5. Lightly toast the cut sides of each baguette section and brush with the remaining oil. Arrange a layer of lettuce leaves, and tomato and onion slices on the bottom half of each section. Top each with 2 slices of pork scallop and a generous spoonful of the Creole Sauce. Cover with the baguette tops and serve immediately.

# Key West Surf and Turf Burgers

## with Avocado, Grapefruit, and Lime Salsa

*This tender beef burger combines the varied flavors of Florida — good-quality beef, fresh seafood, and sun-kissed avocados and grapefruits.*

1 pound 10 ounces fillet or other tender steak, cubed

Salt and freshly ground black pepper

1/2 teaspoon hot pepper sauce (optional)

3 tablespoons olive oil

Curly lettuce

4 slices brioche or good-quality white bread

4 large peeled, cooked shrimp, to garnish

### Avocado, Grapefruit, and Lime Salsa

1 small avocado, peeled, pitted, and diced

Juice of 1 small lime

1 small pink grapefruit, sectioned and cut into small pieces

1/2 papaya, pitted and diced

1 small fresh green chili, deseeded and finely chopped

1 small red onion, finely chopped

1 tablespoon chopped fresh cilantro

1-2 cloves garlic, finely chopped

2 tablespoons extra-virgin olive oil

Salt and freshly ground black pepper

1. Prepare the salsa. Combine all the ingredients in a glass or stainless steel bowl. Cover tightly and refrigerate for at least 2 hours before serving.

2. Put the cubed beef in a food processor and process until coarsely chopped. Transfer to a bowl and season with the salt, pepper, and hot pepper sauce, if using. Toss lightly to blend.

3. Using slightly dampened hands, shape the beef into 4 patties. Arrange on a flat plate, cover tightly with plastic wrap, and refrigerate for at least 1 hour.

4. Heat 2 tablespoons of the olive oil in a large nonstick skillet over a medium–high heat. Add the patties and fry for about 6 minutes, or slightly longer for more well-done burgers, turning once.

5. Meanwhile, lightly toast the brioche or white bread and place a slice on each of 4 plates. Brush each slice with the remaining oil and cover with lettuce. Top each with a burger and a spoonful of the salsa. Garnish each with a shrimp and serve immediately.

# Maryland Crab Burgers
## *with Spicy Sour Cream*

*This recipe is similar to one for old-fashioned crab cakes, but is especially delicious on a toasted burger bun. Fresh white lump crabmeat is the best to use; you can substitute frozen or canned crabmeat, but omit the salt in the recipe.*

1 pound crabmeat, cleaned and flaked

2–3 scallions, finely chopped

1 cup fresh white breadcrumbs

2 tablespoons mayonnaise

1 teaspoon lemon juice

1 tablespoon chopped fresh parsley

1/2 small red bell pepper, finely chopped

Salt

Cayenne pepper, to taste

1 small egg, lightly beaten

Flour for coating

2–3 tablespoons vegetable oil

4 sesame seed burger buns, split and toasted

Lettuce leaves

Tomato slices

Fresh chives, to garnish

### Spicy Sour Cream

4 tablespoons sour cream

1–2 tablespoons mayonnaise

2–3 teaspoons hot or sweet chili sauce, or to taste

Pinch ground cumin

1 tablespoon chopped fresh chives

1. Prepare the sour cream. Combine the sour cream, mayonnaise, chili sauce, cumin, and chives in a small mixing bowl. Cover and refrigerate until ready to serve.

2. In a medium-size bowl, combine the crabmeat, scallions, breadcrumbs, mayonnaise, lemon juice, parsley, red bell pepper, and salt, and cayenne pepper to taste. Stir in the beaten egg. Shape into 4 burgers and dust with flour to coat them evenly.

3. Heat the oil in a heavy-based, preferably nonstick, skillet over a medium–high heat. Add the burgers and cook for 5–8 minutes, turning once, until golden. Remove from the skillet and drain on paper towels.

4. Arrange a few lettuce leaves on the toasted buns. Top each with a burger, tomato slices, and a spoonful of the Spicy Sour Cream. Garnish with chives and serve immediately.

# Creole Shrimp Burgers
## *with Seafood Sauce*

*Creole flavors combine with shrimp to make delicious burgers on toasted sesame buns.*

1½ pounds cooked, peeled shrimp, drained

2–3 scallions, finely chopped

½ red bell pepper, finely chopped

1–2 cloves garlic, chopped

1 teaspoon cornstarch

1 egg white

1 teaspoon salt

1 teaspoon sugar

½ teaspoon hot chili sauce, or hot pepper sauce, to taste

Sesame seeds for coating

Vegetable oil for frying

4 sesame seed burger buns, lightly toasted

Lettuce leaves

Sliced celery

## Seafood Sauce

5 tablespoons mayonnaise

1 scallion, finely chopped

1–2 teaspoons sweet or hot chili sauce, or to taste

1 tablespoon lime or lemon juice

Dash Worcestershire sauce

1. Prepare the sauce. Combine the mayonnaise, scallion, chili sauce, lime or lemon juice, and Worcestershire sauce in a small bowl. Cover and refrigerate until ready to serve.

2. Pat the shrimp dry with paper towels and place them in the bowl of a food processor with the scallion, red bell pepper, garlic, cornstarch, egg white, salt, sugar, and the chili sauce.

*ABOVE: A 1940s matchbook advertising Famous Subway Hamburgers of Shreveport, Louisiana.*

Process until a smooth paste is formed, scraping down the side of the bowl.

3. Shape the mixture into 4 balls. Roll the balls in the seeds to coat, flattening them. Refrigerate for 30 minutes.

4. Heat about ½ inch of oil in a large skillet over a medium–high heat until very hot, but not smoking. Fry the burgers for 2–3 minutes, turning once.

5. Arrange a few lettuce leaves and celery slices on the bun bottoms. Top each with a burger and a little more sliced celery, spoon over a little of the Seafood Sauce, and serve immediately.

# Black-Eyed Pea Burgers

## with Caramelized Red Onions

*Black-eyed peas are a Southern favorite, and they make a delicious base for a very substantial burger.*

1 cup black-eyed
  peas, soaked overnight,
  or 2 x 14-ounce cans
  black-eyed peas
6 tablespoons vegetable oil
1 red onion, chopped
1 red bell pepper, chopped
1 fresh green chili, deseeded
  and chopped

1–2 cloves garlic, crushed
1/2 teaspoon dried thyme
1 tablespoon tomato
  paste
Salt and freshly ground
  black pepper
Cornmeal for coating
Sour cream
Cornbread, to serve

### Caramelized Red Onions

3 tablespoons butter or
  vegetable oil
4 red onions, thinly sliced
1/2 teaspoon dried thyme

1–2 teaspoons balsamic
  or red wine vinegar
1 tablespoon brown sugar
4 tablespoons vegetable
  stock

A TASTY SNACK

1. Prepare the caramelized onions. In a large heavy-based skillet, heat the butter or oil over a medium–high heat until foaming. Add the onions and thyme. Cook, stirring, for 3–4 minutes until the onions begin to soften. Add the vinegar, sugar, and stock or water. Reduce the heat and cook gently for about 20 minutes, stirring occasionally, until the sauce is caramelized and syrupy. Remove from the heat and keep warm in a moderately hot oven; alternatively, let cool and reheat to serve.

2. Drain and rinse the peas well. Put in a medium-size saucepan, cover with cold water, and bring to a boil over a medium–high heat. Reduce the heat to low and simmer for 45–55 minutes, until tender. Drain well and transfer to a large bowl. Alternatively, drain and rinse the canned peas.

3. Meanwhile, heat 2 tablespoons of the oil in a large skillet over a medium heat. Add the onion, red bell pepper, chili, garlic, and dried thyme. Cook for about 7 minutes, until tender. Stir in the tomato paste, then remove the skillet from the heat.

4. Put half the black-eyed peas in the bowl of a food processor with half the vegetable mixture. Process to a rough purée. Stir in the remaining cooked vegetables and peas, and season well with salt and pepper. Shape the mixture into 4 patties.

5. Put the cornmeal in a shallow dish or plate and dip the patties in, one at a time, to coat evenly. Refrigerate the patties for 30 minutes.

6. Heat about 4 tablespoons of the oil in a heavy-based skillet over a medium–high heat. Add the patties and cook for 6–8 minutes, until golden, carefully turning once. Remove and drain on paper towels.

7. Arrange each burger on a slice of cornbread. Top each with some caramelized onions and a spoonful of sour cream, and serve immediately.

# St. Louis Lentil Burgers
## with Warm Tomato and Olive Salad

*Many hamburger historians cite the 1904 World's Fair in St. Louis as one of the first big debuts of the hamburger. This lentil burger comes a long way from the original, but will appeal to vegetarians.*

1½ cups Puy or brown lentils, rinsed

4 tablespoons olive oil

1 small onion, finely chopped

½ red bell pepper, diced

½ yellow bell pepper, diced

2 cloves garlic, finely chopped

½ cup toasted and finely chopped walnut halves

2 tablespoons bottled pesto sauce

Salt and freshly ground black pepper

Lettuce leaves

4 slices white sesame bread, lightly toasted

Fresh basil sprigs, to garnish

### Warm Tomato and Olive Salad

3 tablespoons extra-virgin olive oil

1-2 cloves garlic, finely chopped

6 ripe plum tomatoes, deseeded and chopped

⅓ cup kalamata olives, pitted and coarsely chopped

2 tablespoons shredded fresh basil

2 tablespoons balsamic vinegar

Freshly ground black pepper

1. Put the lentils in a large saucepan and cover with cold water. Bring to a boil over a high heat, then reduce the heat and simmer for about 30 minutes, until tender. Drain and rinse under cold running water and set aside.

2. Heat 2 tablespoons of the olive oil in a large skillet over a medium–high heat. Add the onion and red and yellow bell pepper, and cook for 3–4 minutes until softened. Stir in the garlic and cook for 1 minute more. Remove from the heat.

3. Put half the lentils in the bowl of a food processor. Add half the walnuts and a spoonful of the vegetable mixture. Process for 10–15 seconds; the mixture does not have to be very smooth. Transfer to a large mixing bowl and combine well with the remaining lentils, vegetables, and the pesto. Season with salt and pepper. Shape the mixture into 4 patties, cover firmly, and refrigerate for 30 minutes.

4. Meanwhile, prepare the salad. Heat 2 tablespoons of the olive oil in a saucepan over a medium–heat. Add the garlic and cook for 1–2 minutes, until softened and fragrant, but not browned. Stir in the tomatoes and cook for 2–3 minutes, until warm. Remove from the heat and stir in the olives, basil, and vinegar, and season with black pepper. Pour onto a plate and drizzle with the remaining oil. Keep warm or let cool to room temperature.

5. Preheat the oven to 350°F. Heat the remaining oil in a clean skillet over a medium–high heat until very hot. Add the patties and cook for 3–4 minutes until golden, turning once. Transfer the burgers to a greased foil-lined baking sheet and bake for 8–10 minutes, until crisp and browned. Line each toast slice with lettuce leaves, and top with a burger and a little of the Warm Tomato and Olive Salad. Garnish the burgers with basil and serve immediately.

# Sloppy Joe Burgers
## *with Sautéed Potatoes*

*BELOW: A Wendy's promotional toy truck. David Thomas opened the first Wendy's in 1969.*

*A sloppy joe is a traditional childhood favorite, and here it is brought up to date and served like a burger.*

2 tablespoons vegetable oil

1 large onion, finely chopped

1¹/2 cups chopped mushrooms

1 pound 2 ounces ground beef (90% lean)

1 tablespoon flour

1/2 bouillon cube (optional)

1 cup strained Italian tomatoes (pasata), or tomato sauce

1–2 tablespoons Worcestershire sauce

1 teaspoon powdered mustard

1 teaspoon brown sugar

1/4 cup water

1 tomato, deseeded and chopped

1 cup frozen peas

Lettuce leaves

4 burger buns, lightly toasted

Chopped fresh parsley, to garnish

Sautéed Potatoes, see page 90, to serve

1. Heat the oil in a large heavy-based skillet over a medium–hot heat. Add the onion and cook for 4–5 minutes, until softened and lightly colored. Add the mushrooms and cook for 4–5 minutes more. Add the beef, stirring to break it up, and cook for 3–4 minutes, until the meat is completely browned.

2. Sprinkle over the flour and stir the mixture well. Add the bouillon cube, if using, tomato pasata or sauce, Worcestershire sauce, mustard, sugar, and water. Cook for about 10 minutes, until the mixture is thickened. Stir in the chopped tomato and peas, season with salt and pepper, and cook for 5 minutes more.

3. Arrange the lettuce leaves on the toasted bun bottoms, forming a little cup shape. Fill each cup with the meat mixture, garnish with parsley, and serve immediately with the Sautéed Potatoes.

# The Minnesota Meatball Burger
## with Dill and Mushroom Sauce

*This recipe owes its inspiration to the tiny meatballs made popular by the Scandinavian immigrants who settled in this area of the United States.*

1/4 cup butter

1 small onion, finely chopped

1 cup fresh white breadcrumbs

1 cup milk or light cream

12 ounces ground beef (90% lean)

4 ounces ground veal

4 ounces ground pork

1 egg, lightly beaten

4 tablespoons chopped fresh dill

Salt and freshly ground black pepper

2 tablespoons vegetable oil

1/2 cup thinly sliced mushrooms

1 tablespoon flour

1/4 cup dry white wine

2 cups sour cream

1 tablespoon capers, drained and rinsed

4 slices rye bread, toasted

Fresh dill sprigs, to garnish

Lingonberry sauce or cranberry sauce, to serve (optional)

1. Heat half the butter in a heavy-based skillet over a medium–high heat until foaming. Reserve 1 tablespoon of the chopped onion for the sauce and add the rest to the skillet. Cook for 2–3 minutes until softened, stirring frequently. Transfer to a bowl and let cool.

2. Stir the breadcrumbs and milk or cream into the bowl, and let stand for 3–4 minutes until the liquid is absorbed. Crumble in the ground meats, then add the beaten egg, half the dill, and season with salt and pepper. Using a wooden spoon or fingers, stir the mixture until completely blended. Shape into 4 patties. Cover and refrigerate for 30 minutes.

3. Heat the remaining butter and the oil in a clean skillet over a medium–high heat. Add the patties and cook for 6–8 minutes, turning once, until crisp and golden. Remove from the skillet and drain on paper towels.

4. Add the remaining onion and the mushrooms to the skillet, and stir well. Sprinkle the flour into the pan and stir well. Cook for 1 minute. Pour in the wine, and beat or stir vigorously until the mixture thickens. Stir in the sour cream and cook for 2–3 minutes, but do not boil or the sour cream may curdle. Stir in the remaining chopped dill and the capers. Season with salt and pepper, and cook for 1 minute more.

5. Arrange the meatball patties on the toast slices and spoon over the sauce. Garnish with dill and serve immediately with lingonberry or cranberry sauce, if desired.

# The Calgary Cheeseburger

*This is the classic American cheeseburger — perfect indoors or out, broiled or grilled. Make the burgers thick, and eat them rare and juicy!*

1¹/₂ pounds ground chuck steak (80% lean)

Salt and freshly ground black pepper

4 thick slices sharp cheddar cheese

4 sesame seed buns, split and lightly toasted

Vegetable oil for brushing

Lettuce leaves

Sliced tomatoes and onions

Ketchup, mustard, or other favorite condiments

*ABOVE: The first Wimpy Grill – named for the cartoon character J. Wellington Wimpy – opened in Indiana in the mid-'30s.*

1. Prepare an outdoor charcoal, gas, or electric grill, or preheat an oven broiler. Put the ground beef in a mixing bowl, and season well with salt and pepper. Lightly mix together with a fork or the fingers, and then shape into 4 patties.

2. Arrange the patties on an oiled rack, or on a greased foil-lined broiler pan. Cook for 8–10 minutes, or longer for more well-done burgers, turning once. Two minutes before the end of the cooking time, top each burger with a slice of cheddar cheese and continue grilling or broiling until the cheese has melted.

3. Arrange lettuce leaves and sliced tomatoes and onions on the bun bottoms. Top each with a burger and serve immediately with ketchup, mustard, or other condiments.

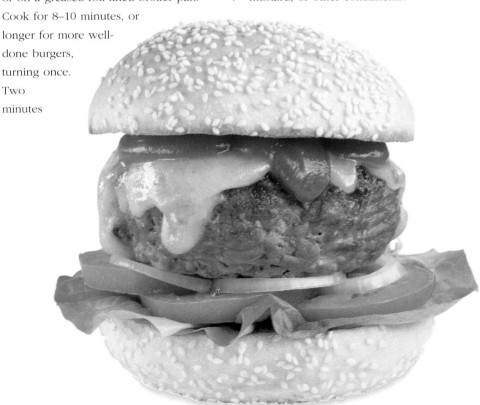

# The Chicago Beef Burger
## *with Beer-Battered Onion Rings*

*Chicago was famous for its meat-packing houses and even more famous for great steaks. This burger uses good-quality sirloin.*

1 pound 10 ounces sirloin, trimmed and cut into small pieces

2 tablespoons beer or soda water

2–3 dashes hot pepper sauce

Salt and freshly ground black pepper

2–3 tablespoons olive or vegetable oil

Lettuce leaves

4 burger buns, split and lightly toasted

Ketchup or other favorite condiments

### Beer-Battered Onion Rings

Vegetable oil for deep-frying

1 1/2 cups flour

2 teaspoons salt

Ground white or black pepper

1/2 cup beer

2 large onions, thinly sliced

1. Prepare the onion rings. Heat about 3 inches of the vegetable oil in a large saucepan or wok to 350°F, or until a small cube of bread turns golden in about 20 seconds. In a large shallow dish, combine the flour, salt, and pepper. Slowly beat in enough beer to make a thin batter.

2. Working in batches, dip a few onion rings into the batter, then slowly lower them into the hot oil. Fry the onions for about 2 minutes, until crisp and golden. Remove with a slotted spoon or wire skimmer and drain on paper towels. Repeat with the remaining onion. Keep the fried onion rings warm in a moderately hot oven.

3. Put the beef in the bowl of a food processor and process until well chopped. Transfer to a bowl. Add the beer or soda water and the hot pepper sauce. Season with salt and pepper, and shape the mixture into 4 patties.

4. Heat the oil in a large heavy-based skillet over a medium–high heat. Add the patties and cook for 7–9 minutes, or longer for more well-done burgers, turning once. Line the bun bottoms with lettuce, top each with a burger and ketchup or other condiments, and serve immediately with the Beer–Battered Onion Rings.

# Veal Burgers
## *with Dried Apricot Relish*

*Because ground veal is generally leaner, a little avocado is added in this recipe to provide extra moisture and creaminess.*

1 tablespoon freshly squeezed lemon juice

1 pound 5 ounces ground veal

1 clove garlic, crushed

Salt and freshly ground black pepper

2–3 tablespoons vegetable oil

Watercress

4 slices white bread, lightly toasted

Fresh mint sprigs, to garnish

### Dried Apricot Relish

1 ripe avocado, halved, pitted, and peeled

2–3 tablespoons freshly squeezed lemon juice

2 scallions, finely chopped

1/2 cup diced ready-to-eat dried apricots

2 fresh apricots (4 ounces in weight), pitted, peeled, and finely chopped

1 clove garlic, crushed

1 tablespoon light brown sugar

1 tablespoon olive oil

1/2 teaspoon ground cinnamon

1/2-inch piece fresh ginger, grated

1 tablespoon chopped fresh mint

Freshly ground black pepper

1. Prepare the relish. Dice half the peeled avocado and put in a bowl with 2 tablespoons of the lemon juice. Toss well. Add the scallions, diced dried apricots, fresh apricots, garlic, brown sugar, oil, cinnamon, ginger, and mint. Toss well, season with pepper, and add a little more lemon juice to taste. Cover and refrigerate until ready to serve.

2. In a large bowl, mash the remaining avocado with a fork. Sprinkle with 1 tablespoon of lemon juice and stir. Add the veal and garlic, and season with salt and pepper. Shape into 4 patties.

3. Heat the oil in a large heavy-based skillet over a medium–high heat. Add the patties and cook for 5–6 minutes, turning once. Remove and drain on paper towels.

4. Arrange a few watercress leaves on the toast slices, and top each with a burger and a spoonful of the apricot relish. Garnish with mint and serve immediately.

Original double-deck Hamburger with Cheese
© 1936 BOB WIAN

# Canadian Ice Burgers
## with Ski-Pole Fries

*This simple method uses a little crushed ice, which melts as the burger cooks and keeps the lean beef moist.*

1 pound 10 ounces ground beef (90% lean)

Salt and freshly ground black pepper

Few dashes hot pepper sauce

4 tablespoons crushed ice

Lettuce leaves

4 burger buns, split and lightly toasted

Sliced onion and dill pickles

Ketchup, mustard, or condiments of your choice

Ski-Pole Fries, see page 91, to serve

1. Prepare an outdoor charcoal, gas, or electric grill, or preheat an oven broiler. Put the beef in a large bowl and season with the salt, pepper, and hot pepper sauce. Toss lightly with a fork or fingers to combine. Add the crushed ice and lightly toss the mixture again. Quickly shape the mixture into 4 patties.

2. Arrange the patties on an oiled rack, or on a greased foil-lined broiler pan. Cook on the grill or under the broiler for 8–10 minutes, or longer for more well-done burgers, turning once.

*ABOVE: A plastic "Big Boy" promotional figure dating from the mid-'60s. By 1950, Big Boy franchises could be found in many regions of the U.S.A.*

3. Arrange the lettuce leaves on the bun bottoms. Top each with a burger, onion slices, sliced pickles, and condiments of your choice. Serve with the fries.

# New Wave Castle Burgers

*The first White Castle hamburger restaurant opened in Wichita, Kansas, in 1921. This New Wave burger is a hearty variation on the original thin beef patty.*

1 pound 10 ounces ground
   beef (80%–90% lean)
Salt and freshly ground
   black pepper
Few dashes Worcestershire
   sauce
1 tablespoon Dijon mustard
1 small onion, finely chopped
1/2 cup crumbled
   blue cheese

4 tablespoons Spicy
   Hamburger Relish, see
   page 87, or tomato
   chutney
Lettuce leaves
4 burger buns, split and
   lightly toasted
Sliced tomatoes and red
   onions
Favorite salad dressing
   (optional)

1. Put the ground beef in a bowl and season with salt, pepper, and the Worcestershire sauce. Toss lightly with a fork or the fingers to combine. Shape into 8 equally sized patties. Using a small spoon, press an indentation in the center of 4 of the patties to make a shallow well.

2. Spread a little mustard in each indentation and sprinkle one-quarter of the chopped onions over each one. Divide the blue cheese evenly between the wells, and top each with a spoonful of relish or chutney. Place the remaining 4 patties over the filled patties, and pinch the edges together to completely enclose the filling, making 4 stuffed burgers. Cover and refrigerate for 20 minutes.

3. Prepare an outside charcoal, gas, or electric grill, or preheat a broiler. Arrange the patties on an oiled rack, or a greased foil-lined broiler pan. Cook for 8–10 minutes, or longer for more well-done burgers if desired, turning once; the cheesy filling should be melted inside the burgers.

4. Arrange a few lettuce leaves on the bun bottoms and top each with a burger. Add some slices of tomato and onion. Spoon over a little extra relish or chutney, or drizzle the burgers with a favorite salad dressing, and serve immediately.

*FAR LEFT and LEFT: Customers can still "Buy 'em by the sackful" at White Castle. The packaging design (far left) dates from 1931.*

# THE SOUTHWEST

# Southwest Lamb Burgers
## with Grilled Bell Pepper Salad

*The competition between cattle and sheep farmers in the old West is over — lamb makes juicy, delicious burgers, which taste just as good as beef. Ground lamb from supermarkets can be used, but the shoulder meat is particularly sweet.*

1 clove garlic, finely chopped

1 tablespoon chopped fresh rosemary

1³/₄ pounds boned lamb shoulder, trimmed and cut into small pieces

3 tablespoons olive oil

Salt and freshly ground black pepper

4 burger buns, split and lightly toasted

Lettuce leaves

### Grilled Bell Pepper Salad

1 red bell pepper

1 yellow bell pepper

1 orange bell pepper

1 red onion, thinly sliced

1/2 cup black olives

2–3 tablespoons balsamic vinegar

Salt and freshly ground black pepper

2 tablespoons extra-virgin olive oil

1. Preheat an oven broiler and arrange the bell peppers on a greased foil-lined broiler pan. Grill the peppers under the broiler, turning to char evenly, until each side is slightly blistered, but not completely black. Remove from the heat and place an upturned bowl over the peppers to let the steam to loosen the skins.

2. When cool enough to handle, peel off the skins and cut the flesh into slices, removing the seeds and core. Arrange in a shallow dish with the onion slices, olives, and vinegar. Season with salt and pepper, drizzle with the olive oil, and set aside.

3. With a food processor running, drop the cloves of garlic through the feed tube, then drop in the rosemary. Process until finely chopped. Add the lamb and process until finely chopped. Drizzle over 1 tablespoon of olive oil, season with salt and pepper, and process briefly to blend. Shape the mixture into 4 patties.

4. Heat the remaining olive oil in a large heavy-based skillet over a medium–high heat. Add the patties and cook for 6–8 minutes, turning once, until crisp and browned. Line each bun bottom with lettuce, top with some of the Grilled Bell Pepper Salad and a burger, and serve immediately.

*LEFT: Placards such as this one were mass-produced in the '40s for use by burger restaurants and diners across the land.*

# Tex-Mex Burgers
## with Tortillas and Guacamole

*The delicious flavors of ripe tomatoes, cilantro, lime, avocado, and blisteringly hot chilies are evident in this Mexican-influenced burger.*

1¹/2 pounds ground beef
   (85% lean)
1 small onion, grated
1 clove garlic, finely chopped
¹/2 teaspoon chili powder
1 teaspoon ground cumin
1 cup grated cheddar or
   Monteray Jack cheese

Vegetable oil for frying
2 flour tortillas, cut in half
Shredded lettuce
Sliced tomatoes
Fresh cilantro sprigs,
   to garnish
Commercial variety of
   tomato-chili salsa,
   to serve

### Guacamole

1 medium ripe avocado,
   halved, pitted, and peeled
1 medium ripe tomato,
   skinned, deseeded, and
   chopped
1 small red onion, chopped
1 clove garlic, finely chopped

1-2 small fresh green
   chilies, deseeded and
   finely chopped
Grated zest and juice of
   2 small limes
2 tablespoons chopped
   fresh cilantro

1. Prepare the Guacamole. Mash the avocado in a medium-size bowl. Add the remaining ingredients and mix to combine well. Cover and refrigerate.

2. In a medium-size bowl, combine the beef, onion, garlic, chili powder, cumin, and half the grated cheese. Shape the mixture into 4 patties and set aside.

3. Heat about ³/4 inch of oil in a large heavy-based skillet over a medium–hot heat. Place a tortilla half on a clean work counter and sprinkle 1 tablespoon of grated cheese on the bottom half. Fold over the top half to form a triangle. Press down firmly to stick the tortilla together. Repeat with the remaining 3 tortilla halves. Slide each tortilla triangle into the oil and fry for about 2 minutes,

turning once, until golden. Drain on paper towels and keep warm in the oven.

4. Pour off all but 2 tablespoons of the oil from the skillet and add the patties. Cook for 6–8 minutes, or longer for a more well-done burger, turning once. Place each warm tortilla triangle on a plate and top with some shredded lettuce, sliced tomatoes, and any leftover cheese. Arrange a burger on each and top with the Guacamole. Garnish with sprigs of cilantro and serve immediately with the salsa.

# Chili Steak Burgers
## *with Marinated Red Cabbage*

*These burgers are especially good when charcoal-grilled outdoors. If possible, prepare the red cabbage a day ahead of time.*

4 tablespoons vegetable oil
1 small onion, finely chopped
1 small green bell pepper, finely diced
1 small red bell pepper, finely diced
1–2 cloves garlic, finely chopped
1 teaspoon ground cumin
1/2 teaspoon crushed hot peppers
Salt
1 pound 10 ounces tender beef, such as topside, cut into small pieces
Lettuce leaves
4 burger buns, split and toasted

## Marinated Red Cabbage

1 small head red cabbage, cored and thinly shredded
1 small red onion, thinly sliced
3/4 cup sherry or red wine vinegar
1/4 cup virgin olive oil
2 tablespoons vegetable oil
2 tablespoons brown sugar
1 teaspoon mustard seeds, lightly crushed
1 tablespoon powdered mustard
Salt and freshly ground black pepper

1. Prepare the cabbage. Put the cabbage and onions in a large stainless steel or glass bowl and toss well to combine. Put the remaining ingredients in a small saucepan over a high heat and bring to a boil. Remove from the heat and pour over the cabbage and onions.

Gently press the cabbage and onions under the liquid, then let cool. Cover and refrigerate for several hours, or overnight.

2. Heat 2 tablespoons of the oil in a large heavy-based skillet over a medium–high heat. Add the onions and bell peppers, and cook for 3–4 minutes, until beginning to soften. Add the garlic, cumin, and crushed hot peppers, and season with salt. Cook for 1 minute more. Transfer the vegetable mixture to a large bowl and let cool.

3. Put the beef in the bowl of a food processor and process until coarsely chopped. Add the beef to the cooled vegetable mixture and toss to combine well. Shape into 4 patties.

4. Heat the remaining oil in a clean skillet over a medium–high heat. Add the beef patties and cook for 6–8 minutes, or longer for more well-done burgers, turning once. Arrange lettuce leaves on the toasted bun bottoms, top each with a burger and a little of the Marinated Red Cabbage, and serve immediately.

# Santa Fe Fajita-Style Chicken Burgers

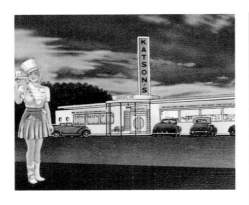

*These burgers owe their inspiration to Mexican fajitas, but they are cooked like burgers.*

1 pound 10 ounces ground chicken

1 tablespoon vegetable oil

1 small red onion, finely chopped

1 small red bell pepper finely chopped

1 clove garlic, crushed

1–2 tablespoons lime juice

1 tablespoon chopped fresh cilantro

1 teaspoon hot chili powder

Salt

4 flour tortillas

Shredded lettuce

Chopped tomatoes

Sliced avocado

Spicy Hamburger Relish, see page 87, or a commercial brand of tomato-chili salsa, to serve

Fresh cilantro sprigs, to garnish

Guacamole, see page 54, to serve (optional)

1. Prepare an outdoor charcoal, gas, or electric grill, or preheat an oven broiler. In a large bowl, toss the chicken with the oil, onion, red bell pepper, garlic, lime juice, cilantro, and chili powder, and season with salt. Shape the mixture into 4 oval patties.

2. Arrange the patties on an oiled rack, or on a greased foil-lined broiler pan. Cook for 6–8 minutes, until cooked through and well colored. Wrap the tortillas in foil and heat on the side of the barbecue for 3–4 minutes; alternatively, wrap the tortillas in plastic wrap and microwave on high at 30-second intervals until warm.

3. Lay a warm tortilla on a clean work counter and put some lettuce, tomatoes, avocado, and hamburger relish or salsa on one-third. Top with a burger and fold the tortilla around the burger, tucking in the bottom. Repeat with the remaining 3 burgers. Alternatively, let each person assemble his or her own burger. Garnish the burgers with cilantro and serve immediately with the Guacamole.

# Tucson Turkey Burgers
## with Salsa

1. Prepare an outdoor charcoal, gas, or electric grill, or preheat an oven broiler. In a large bowl, toss the turkey with the salsa, cilantro, and cumin, and season with salt. Shape into 4 patties.

2. Arrange the patties on an oiled rack, or on a greased foil-lined broiler pan. Cook for 8–10 minutes until well colored and cooked through, turning once.

3. Two minutes before the end of the cooking time, arrange a few slices of avocado on each burger and sprinkle with the cheese. Continue grilling or broiling until the cheese has melted.

4. Arrange the lettuce leaves on the bun bottoms. Top each with a burger and a spoonful of the tomato–chili salsa, and serve immediately.

*Salsa, a spicy fresh relish made from a variety of ingredients, is widely available from supermarkets. Choose a good-quality commercial brand of tomato-chili salsa for this recipe.*

1¹/₂ pounds ground turkey
³/₄ cup good-quality commercial brand of tomato-chili salsa, well drained
2 tablespoons chopped fresh cilantro
1 teaspoon ground cumin
Salt
1 ripe avocado, peeled, pitted, and thinly sliced

¹/₂ cup grated cheddar or Monteray Jack cheese
Lettuce leaves
4 burger buns, split and toasted
Extra tomato-chili salsa, to serve

# Campfire Burgers
## *with Barbecue Sauce*

*For a real campfire atmosphere, cook these burgers on an outdoor grill.*

1 pound 9 ounces ground
  beef (85% lean)
Salt and freshly ground
  black pepper
3/4 cup Easy Barbecue
  Sauce, see page 89, or a
  good-quality commercial
  variety

Shredded lettuce
4 burger buns, split and
  toasted
Sliced tomatoes and onions
Perfect Fries, see page 91,
  to serve (optional)
Ketchup and mustard, to
  serve (optional)

1. Prepare an outdoor charcoal, gas, or electric grill, or preheat an oven broiler Place the beef in a large bowl. Toss with salt and pepper, and 1–2 tablespoons of barbecue sauce. Shape into 4 burgers.

2. Arrange the burgers on an oiled rack, or a greased foil-lined broiler pan. Cook for 6–8 minutes, brushing generously with barbecue sauce and turning once.

3. Arrange some shredded lettuce on the bun bottoms and top each with a burger and a few slices of tomato and onion. Serve immediately, with Perfect Fries and condiments, if desired.

*ABOVE and LEFT:*
*Prince's restaurants were located in Houston, Beaumont, Dallas, and San Antonio.*

# Texas Beef Burgers

## *with Corn Chips and Cherry Tomato Salsa*

*These burgers are typically Texan — big in size and strong in flavor.*

1 pound 10 ounces ground beef (80% lean)

2 tablespoons good-quality steak sauce

1 teaspoon garlic salt

1/2 teaspoon crushed hot peppers

1 medium onion, thickly sliced

4 burger buns, split and toasted

Fresh cilantro sprigs, to garnish

Corn chips, to serve

### Cherry Tomato Salsa

2 1/2 cups halved cherry tomatoes

1 medium red onion, chopped

1 small red bell pepper, chopped

1–2 small fresh red or green chilies, deseeded and chopped

1 clove garlic, finely chopped

2 tablespoons olive oil

1 tablespoon sunflower oil

Grated zest and juice of 2 limes or small lemons

1 tablespoon brown sugar

1/4 teaspoon ground cinnamon

2 tablespoons chopped fresh cilantro

1. Prepare the salsa. Put all the salsa ingredients in a glass or stainless steel bowl and mix well to combine. Cover and refrigerate for about 2 hours before serving, to allow the flavors to develop.

2. Prepare an outdoor charcoal, gas, or electric grill, or preheat an oven broiler. In a large bowl, toss the beef with the steak sauce, garlic salt, and crushed hot peppers. Shape into 4 patties.

3. Place the patties on an oiled rack, or a greased foil-lined broiler pan. Cook for 6–8 minutes, or longer for a more well-done burger, turning once. Place a few onion slices and a burger on each burger bottom, and top with a little Cherry Tomato Salsa. Garnish with cilantro and serve immediately with the corn chips.

# Roadhouse Double Cheeseburgers
## with Marinated Red Onions

*These burgers make a substantial meal, and the marinated onions are the perfect accompaniment.*

I pound 10 ounces ground
  beef (90% lean)
I small onion, grated
2 cloves garlic, finely
  chopped
I tablespoon chopped fresh
  parsley or basil
3 tablespoons grated
  Parmesan cheese

4 ounces cheddar or
  Monteray Jack cheese,
  cut into I x 1/2 inch
  pieces
Olive oil for brushing
Lettuce leaves
4 burger buns or slices
  of country-style bread,
  toasted
Fresh parsley or basil
  sprigs, to garnish

### Marinated Red Onions

2 red onions, thinly sliced
2 tablespoons cider vinegar
I tablespoon brown sugar

1/4 teaspoon salt
Freshly ground black pepper

1. Prepare the marinated onions. Combine all the ingredients in a small bowl. Cover and refrigerate for 3–4 hours, or overnight.

2. Place the beef in a large bowl, add the onion, garlic, parsley or basil, and Parmesan cheese, and lightly mix to combine. Shape into 8 patties. Place a cube of cheese on 4 of the patties and cover with the remaining patties, sealing the edges and flattening them to make 4 thick burgers.

3. Preheat an oven broiler. Arrange the patties on a greased foil-lined broiler pan and brush the tops with oil. Cook for 6-8 minutes, or longer for a more well-done burger, turning once. Just before the end of the cooking time, top each burger with a few more pieces of cheese and return to the broiler until the cheese has melted.

4. Line lettuce on the bun bottoms and top each with a burger and a little of the marinated onions. Garnish with parsley or basil, and serve immediately.

*RIGHT: The Round-Up Drive-In of Las Vegas, Nevada, claimed the title of "the world's largest drive-in restaurant" in its adverts of the early '50s.*

# Chickpea Burgers
## with Creamy Hummus Dressing

*Here mashed chickpeas are made into a substantial burger, and into hummus, the famous Middle-Eastern dip. Tahini, or sesame paste, is a necessary ingredient for the hummus; it is available from natural food stores, ethnic markets, and some specialty sections in large supermarkets.*

4 tablespoons olive oil

1 onion, finely chopped

2 teaspoons curry powder

1 clove garlic, crushed

1 small red bell pepper, finely chopped

1 small leek, finely chopped

1 cup frozen peas, thawed

1 tomato, skinned, deseeded, and chopped

1/2 teaspoon crushed hot peppers

11-ounce can chickpeas, drained and rinsed

1 cup fresh white breadcrumbs

1 egg, lightly beaten

Salt and freshly ground black pepper

4 pita breads, toasted

Lettuce leaves

Slices of cucumber, onion, and tomato

Cilantro leaves, to garnish

### Creamy Hummus Dressing

11-ounce can chickpeas, drained and rinsed, with liquid reserved

2 cloves garlic, crushed

2 tablespoons lemon juice

2-3 tablespoons tahini

1 teaspoon ground cumin (optional)

Salt and freshly ground black pepper

2-4 tablespoons olive oil

1. Prepare the hummus. Place the chickpeas in the bowl of a food processor and process until smooth, scraping down the side of the bowl as necessary. Add the garlic, lemon juice, tahini, and cumin, if using. Season with salt and pepper, and process again until smooth. With the machine running, slowly pour in the olive oil until well incorporated. If the hummus is too thick, process again with a little of the reserved chickpea liquid. Transfer to a bowl, cover, and refrigerate until ready to serve, or up to 1 week.

2. Heat 2 tablespoons of the olive oil in a large heavy-based skillet over a medium heat. Add the onion and curry powder, and cook for 2–3 minutes. Add the garlic, red bell pepper, leek, peas, tomato, and crushed hot peppers. Cook for 5–7 minutes, until the vegetables are tender. Remove and let cool.

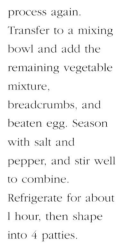

**fat Eddie**

Close Cover Before Striking

3. Put the chickpeas in the bowl of a food processor and process until smooth. Add half the vegetable mixture and process again. Transfer to a mixing bowl and add the remaining vegetable mixture, breadcrumbs, and beaten egg. Season with salt and pepper, and stir well to combine. Refrigerate for about 1 hour, then shape into 4 patties.

4. Heat the remaining oil in a clean skillet over a medium heat. Add the chickpea patties and cook for 6–8 minutes, turning once, until crisp, golden, and heated through.

5. Arrange the lettuce leaves on the pita breads. Layer sliced cucumber, onion, and tomato on each pita, and top with a burger. Spoon a little Creamy Hummus Dressing on each burger, garnish with cilantro leaves, and serve immediately.

# Lamb Burgers
## with Minted Yogurt Dressing

*The lamb is stacked to resemble a burger. If desired, substitute ground lamb, flavored with spices, and cook as for any other burger.*

2 lamb fillets, about
  1 pound 2 ounces each
4 tablespoons olive oil
2 cloves garlic, crushed
1 teaspoon ground cumin
Grated zest and juice of
  1 lemon

Salt and freshly ground
  black pepper
4 slices Greek-style sesame
  bread, or 4 small pita
  breads, toasted
Lettuce leaves
Fresh mint leaves, to garnish

### Greek Salad

1 1/2 cups quartered cherry
  tomatoes
1/2 cup pitted black olives
3 ounces feta cheese, cubed

1/2 teaspoon crushed hot
  peppers
3–4 tablespoons olive oil

### Minted Yogurt Dressing

3/4 cup thick plain yogurt
1 tablespoon extra-virgin
  olive oil
2-inch piece cucumber,
  peeled, deseeded, and
  diced

1 tablespoon chopped
  fresh mint
1/4 teaspoon cumin
1 teaspoon sugar

1. Prepare the dressing. Combine all the ingredients in a small bowl until well blended. Cover and refrigerate until ready to serve.

2. Put the lamb in a shallow dish and pour over the olive oil. Spread the garlic over the lamb, and sprinkle with cumin and the lemon zest and juice. Season with salt and pepper. Cover and marinate for 30 minutes to 2 hours, turning at least once.

3. Prepare an outdoor charcoal, gas, or electric grill, or preheat an oven broiler. Arrange the lamb on an oiled rack, or on a greased foil-lined broiler pan. Cook the fillets for 5–6 minutes, or longer for more well-done lamb, turning once. Transfer to a cutting board, cover loosely with foil, and let rest for 5 minutes.

4. Toss all the ingredients for the salad together in a bowl. Arrange lettuce leaves on the toast slices. Slice the lamb thinly on the diagonal and divide among the burgers. Top with the dressing, garnish with mint, and serve immediately with the salad.

# California-Style Pizza Burgers

*These burgers resemble mini pizzas. If you cannot find ciabatta rolls, use a loaf of ciabatta and toast thick slices.*

8 ounces hot or sweet Italian-style sausage, removed from its casing

1 pound ground beef (85% lean)

2 tablespoons grated Parmesan cheese

1 teaspoon dried oregano

1/2 teaspoon dried thyme

1 clove garlic, crushed

1/3 cup pitted and chopped black olives

1/2 cup bottled or homemade pizza sauce

Freshly ground black pepper

8 slices mozzarella cheese

4 ciabatta rolls, split and toasted

Olive oil

Parmesan shavings, to garnish

Fresh basil leaves, to garnish

1. Crumble the sausage meat into a large mixing bowl, then crumble in the beef. Add the Parmesan cheese, oregano, thyme, garlic, olives, and 1–2 tablespoons of the pizza sauce. Season with pepper. Mix by hand until well blended and the mixture holds together. Shape into 4 patties.

*ABOVE RIGHT: An eye-catching 1950s menu from The Clock Broiler of Southern California.*

2. Prepare an outdoor charcoal, gas, or electric grill, or preheat an oven broiler. Arrange the burgers on an oiled rack, or a greased foil-lined broiler pan. Cook the patties for 8–10 minutes, brushing with the remaining pizza sauce and turning once. Top each burger with 2 slices of mozzarella 1 minute before the end of the cooking time.

3. Arrange the ciabatta roll bottoms on plates and brush with a little olive oil. Divide any remaining pizza sauce between them and top each with a burger. Garnish with shavings of Parmesan and the basil, and serve immediately.

# Tuna Burgers

## with Wasabi Mayonnaise and Pickled Ginger

*This tasty tuna burger is enhanced by Japanese wasabi (green horseradish) and pickled ginger. The condiments can be found in oriental food stores.*

1½ pounds very fresh tuna, cut into pieces

½-inch piece fresh ginger, grated

2 scallions, finely chopped

1 teaspoon rice vinegar

1 tablespoon chopped fresh dill or chives

Salt and freshly ground black pepper

1 tablespoon vegetable oil

1 teaspoon sesame oil

4 sesame seed buns, split and lightly toasted

Thinly sliced cucumber

Pickled ginger

### Wasabi Mayonnaise

2 teaspoons wasabi powder

4 teaspoons cold water

½ cup good-quality commercial mayonnaise

Juice of ½ lemon or lime

1 clove garlic, finely minced

½ teaspoon Japanese soy sauce

1. Prepare the mayonnaise. Put the wasabi powder or paste in a bowl and gradually stir in the water to make a smooth paste. Slowly blend in the mayonnaise, then the remaining ingredients. Cover and refrigerate until ready to serve.

2. Put the tuna in the bowl of a food processor and process until coarsely chopped. Add the ginger, scallion, vinegar, and dill or chives, and process briefly to combine. Season with salt and pepper. Shape into

4 patties. Cover tightly with plastic wrap and refrigerate for at least 1 hour.

3. Heat the oils in a large nonstick skillet over a medium–high heat. Add the patties and cook for 8–10 minutes, turning once, until crisp and browned.

4. Spread the bun bottoms with a little of the Wasabi Mayonnaise and cover with sliced cucumber. Top each with a burger, a little more of the mayonnaise, and a few slices of pickled ginger. Serve immediately.

# Vietnamese Steak Burgers
## with Pickled Cucumber and Carrots

*Many Asian cultures offer a version of these lightly pickled vegetables, which contrast well with the sweetness of the burger. Either Vietnamese or Thai fish sauce can be used.*

2 tablespoons Japanese soy sauce or bottled teriyaki marinade

2 tablespoons water

2 tablespoons light brown sugar

2 tablespoons Vietnamese fish sauce (nuoc nam)

1 onion, finely chopped

1–3 cloves garlic

1/2 teaspoon crushed hot peppers

1 3/4 pounds sirloin steak, cut into small pieces

4 large lettuce leaves

### Pickled Cucumber and Carrots

1/2 cup rice vinegar

1/2 cup warm water

2 tablespoons sugar

1/2 teaspoon salt

2 teaspoons Vietnamese fish sauce (nuoc nam)

1 large cucumber, lightly peeled, deseeded, and cut into julienne strips

2 carrots, cut into julienne strips

1 red onion, thinly sliced

Fresh mint or cilantro leaves

1. Prepare the pickled vegetables. In a large bowl, stir together the vinegar, water, sugar, salt, and fish sauce until the sugar is dissolved. Add the vegetables and herbs, and stir to combine. Cover and refrigerate for 1 hour, or overnight.

2. Put the soy sauce or teriyaki marinade in a small saucepan with the water, sugar, fish sauce, onion, garlic, and crushed hot peppers. Bring to a boil, stirring frequently. Remove from the heat and let cool.

3. Put the steak pieces in the bowl of a food processor and process until finely chopped. Transfer the meat to a bowl and add the cooled soy sauce mixture. Mix by hand to blend and shape into 4 patties.

4. Prepare an outdoor charcoal, gas, or electric grill, or preheat an oven broiler. Arrange the patties on an oiled rack, or a greased foil-lined broiler pan. Cook the patties for 6–8 minutes, or longer for more well-done burgers, turning once. Line 4 plates with lettuce leaves and arrange a burger on each one. Top with the pickled vegetables and serve immediately.

# Tandoori-Style Chicken Burgers

*This spicy chicken burger uses the Asian
flavors of tandoori cooking.*

1/2 cup plain yogurt

1-inch piece fresh
ginger, peeled and grated

2 cloves garlic, crushed

1 tablespoon tandoori powder,
or 2 tablespoons tandoori
curry paste

1 tablespoon brown
sugar

4 boneless, skinless chicken
breasts, about 6 ounces
each, split horizontally to
make 8 slices

4 naan breads, warmed

Lettuce leaves

Sliced tomato and cucumber

Fresh cilantro or mint
leaves

Mango or tomato chutney,
or Indian-style
lime pickle

Minted Yogurt Dressing,
see page 66, to serve

1. Place the yogurt, ginger, garlic, tandoori powder or paste, and sugar in a shallow glass dish. Mix to combine well. Add the chicken breasts and turn to coat evenly. Cover and refrigerate for at least 1 hour, and 2–3 hours if possible.

2. Prepare an outdoor charcoal, gas, or electric grill, or preheat an oven broiler. Arrange the chicken pieces on an oiled rack, or on a greased foil-lined broiler pan. Cook the chicken on the grill or under a broiler for 7–10 minutes, turning once, until well colored and just cooked through.

3. Arrange the warm naan bread on plates. Top one-half of each bread with lettuce leaves, tomato and cucumber slices, and a chicken burger. Finish with a spoonful of chutney or lime pickle, add a few cilantro or mint leaves, and fold over the naan bread to enclose the filling. Serve immediately with the Minted Yogurt Dressing.

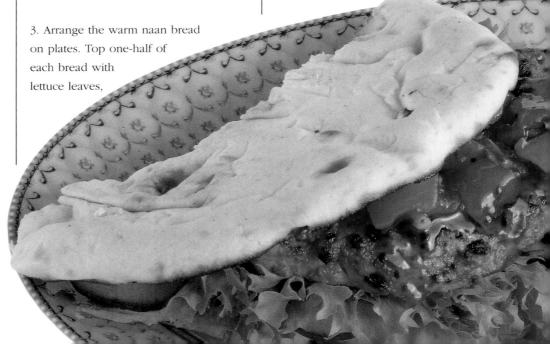

# Napa Valley Bistro Burgers

*This burger resembles the grilled goat cheese salad served in many bistro-style restaurants. It is popular because the flavors and textures go so well together.*

1 pound 9 ounces ground lamb or beef (90% lean)

3 tablespoons bottled pesto sauce

2 tablespoons grated Parmesan cheese

Salt and freshly ground black pepper

Olive oil for brushing

4 ounces goat cheese, cut into 8 rounds

4 burger buns, split and lightly toasted

Mixed salad leaves

Creamy Vinaigrette, see page 87

2 tablespoons pine nuts, lightly toasted

1. Prepare an outdoor charcoal, gas, or electric grill, or preheat an oven broiler. Place the lamb or beef, pesto, and Parmesan in a large bowl. Season with salt and black pepper, and mix together to combine well. Shape into 4 patties and brush with olive oil.

2. Arrange the burgers on an oiled rack, or on a greased foil-lined broiler pan. Cook for 8–10 minutes until well browned, but still pink inside, turning once. Top each burger with 2 slices of goat cheese about 1 minute before the end of the cooking time and let soften.

3. Brush the bun bottoms with olive oil, toss the salad leaves with the vinaigrette, and arrange the leaves on the buns. Top each with a burger, sprinkle over the pine nuts, and serve immediately.

# Honolulu Teriyaki Burgers
## with Tropical Fruit Salsa

*The tropical ingredients in this recipe make a uniquely delicious burger. The fruit salsa completes the meal.*

1/2 cup bottled teriyaki marinade

1 small onion, grated

2 cloves garlic, crushed

1 tablespoon brown sugar

2 tablespoons chopped fresh cilantro or mint

1-inch piece fresh ginger, peeled and finely chopped

1 teaspoon sesame oil

Freshly ground black pepper

1 pound 2 ounces ground beef (90% lean)

16 ounces ground pork

2 tablespoons vegetable oil

Lettuce leaves

4 slices sesame bread, toasted

Fresh cilantro or mint sprigs, to garnish

### Tropical Fruit Salsa

4 tablespoons coconut milk

Grated zest and juice of 1/2 lime

1/2 small fresh red or green chili, deseeded and finely chopped

1 teaspoon brown sugar

1 small pineapple, peeled, cored, and cut into small chunks

1 small ripe mango, peeled and diced

1 small medium papaya, peeled, deseeded, and diced

1 kiwi fruit, peeled and sliced

1 tablespoon chopped fresh cilantro or mint

1. Prepare the salsa. Beat the coconut milk, lime zest and juice, chili, and brown sugar in a large bowl. Reserve about 1 cup of pineapple chunks for the burgers, and add the remaining pineapple to the bowl with the mango, papaya, kiwi, and cilantro or mint. Toss well to combine. Cover and refrigerate until ready to serve.

2. Combine the teriyaki marinade, onion, garlic, brown sugar, cilantro or mint, ginger, and sesame oil in a large bowl.

Season with pepper. Reserve about 4 tablespoons of the marinade mixture and set aside. Crumble in the ground beef and pork, and use a fork to mix lightly until well blended. Shape into 4 patties.

3. Heat the vegetable oil in a large, nonstick skillet over a medium–hot heat. Add the patties and cook for 6–8 minutes, or slightly longer for more well-done burgers, turning once. Brush with a little reserved marinade as they cook. Line the toast slices with lettuce leaves and top each with a burger.

4. Add the reserved marinade to the skillet with the reserved pineapple chunks, and toss to coat with the marinade. Cook for 1–2 minutes, until the pineapple is glazed and hot. Top each burger with a few glazed pineapple chunks and garnish with the cilantro or mint. Serve immediately with the Tropical Fruit Salsa.

*LEFT: Bob Wian started a hamburger revolution when he invented the "double-deck" burger in the late '30s.*

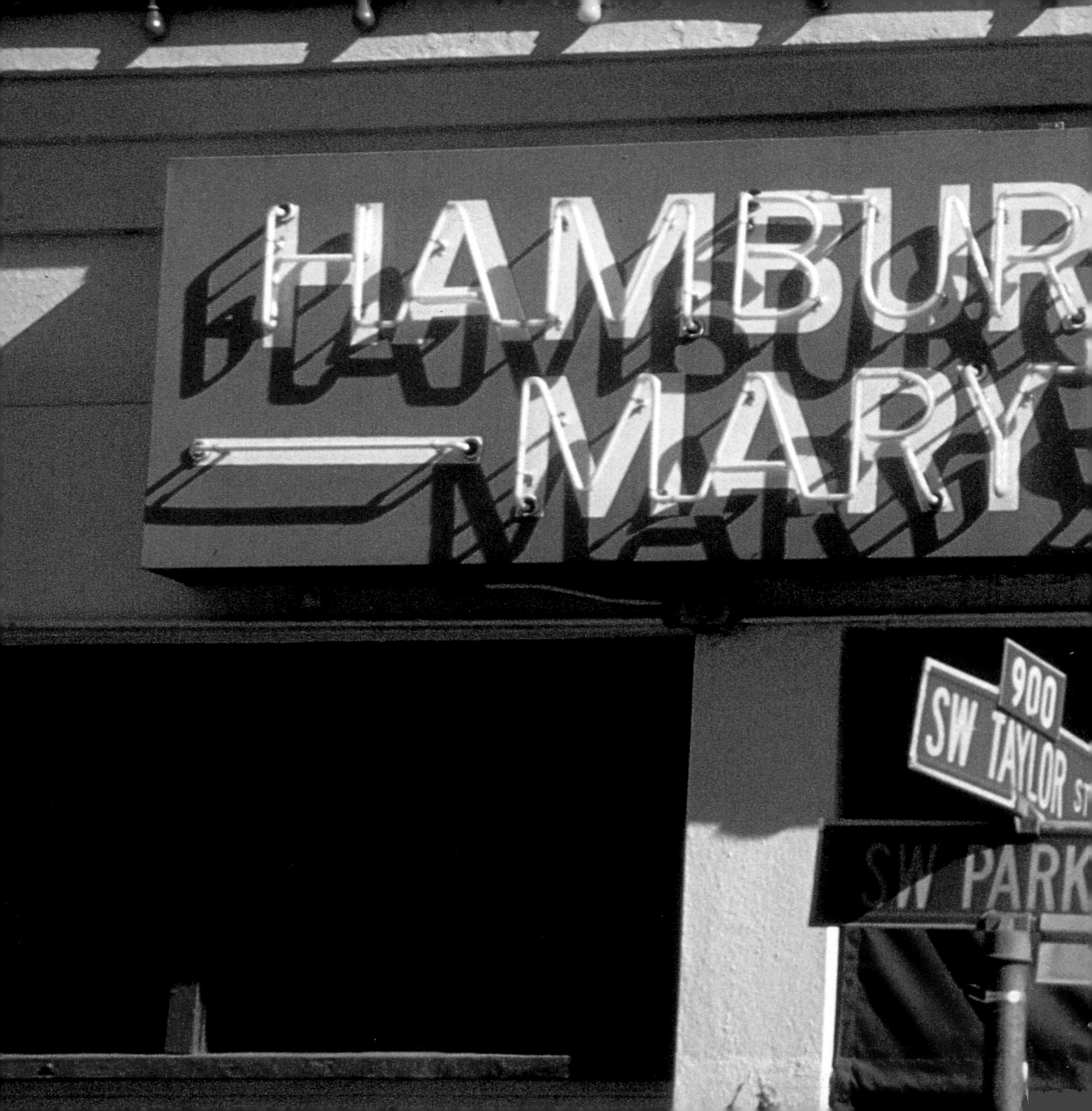
HAMBUR
MARY
900
SW TAYLOR ST
SW PARK

# THE NORTHWEST & MOUNTAIN STATES

# Salmon Burgers
## with Horseradish Mayonnaise and Potato and Fennel Salad

*This simple burger uses the best of North America's Pacific salmon. The tangy horseradish mayonnaise complements the flavor, but be sure to use grated horseradish and not the creamed variety. Serve with Perfect Fries, see page 91, if you prefer.*

1¹/₂ pounds fresh salmon, cut into pieces
1 tablespoon mayonnaise
1 tablespoon Dijon mustard
1 tablespoon chopped fresh dill or chives
Salt and freshly ground black pepper

2–3 tablespoons vegetable oil
Lettuce leaves
4 slices brioche or challah bread, toasted
Fresh dill sprigs, to garnish

## Potato and Fennel Salad

4 tablespoons mayonnaise
1 tablespoon milk
1 tablespoon Dijon mustard
1 tablespoon cider vinegar
1 tablespoon chopped fresh dill

2 medium large potatoes, cooked, peeled, and diced
1 large Florence fennel bulb, cored and chopped
1 small red onion, chopped

## Horseradish Mayonnaise

3–4 tablespoons mayonnaise
2 tablespoons grated horseradish

1 teaspoon chopped fresh dill

1. Prepare the mayonnaise. Combine all the ingredients in a small mixing bowl. Cover and refrigerate until ready to serve.

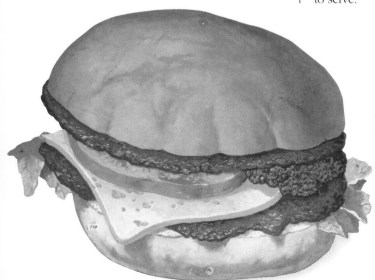

*LEFT: A painting of a hamburger that used to be on display in the now-defunct Andy's Cafe in Seattle, Washington.*

2. Prepare the salad. Combine the mayonnaise, milk, mustard, vinegar, and dill in a large bowl. Add the potatoes, fennel, and onion, and toss to combine. Cover and refrigerate until ready to serve.

3. Put the salmon pieces in the bowl of a food processor and process until finely chopped. Transfer to a large bowl. Stir in the mayonnaise, mustard, and dill or chives, and season with salt and pepper. Shape into 4 patties, cover, and refrigerate for 2 hours, or overnight.

4. Heat 2 tablespoons of the oil in a large heavy-based skillet over a medium–high heat, or oil a black iron stove-top grill pan. Cook the patties for 8–10 minutes, turning once, until crisp and well colored.

5. Arrange lettuce leaves on each slice of toast, and top with a burger and a spoonful of the Horseradish Mayonnaise. Garnish with dill and serve immediately with the Potato and Fennel Salad.

# Northwest Trout Burgers
## with Sun-dried Tomato Mayonnaise

*The trout streams of the Northwest produce wonderful fish. Use the freshest fish possible for the best flavor.*

1¹/₂ pounds cooked fresh trout, flaked

2 scallions, finely chopped

2 cups fresh white breadcrumbs

I egg, beaten

2 tablespoons mayonnaise

2 tablespoons snipped fresh chives

Salt and freshly ground black pepper

1–2 tablespoons lemon juice

Dry breadcrumbs for coating

2 tablespoons butter

I tablespoon oil

Mixed lettuce leaues, to serve

### Sun-dried Tomato Mayonnaise

4 tablespoons mayonnaise

2–3 sun-dried tomatoes, chopped

2–3 black oliues, pitted and chopped

1. Put the flaked fish in a large bowl and toss with the scallion and breadcrumbs. Make a well in the center, and add the egg, mayonnaise, chives, and lemon juice, and season with salt and pepper. Using a fork, lightly beat together to mix, gradually adding in the trout mixture until completely blended. Shape into 4 patties.

2. Spread the dried breadcrumbs on a shallow dish or plate and dip in the trout patties to lightly and evenly coat. Place on a plate and refrigerate for at least I hour.

3. Meanwhile, prepare the mayonnaise. Place the mayonnaise and sun-dried tomatoes in a food processor or blender and process until smooth. Transfer to a bowl and stir in the olives. Cover and refrigerate until ready to serve.

4. Heat the butter and oil in a large heavy-based skillet. Add the patties and cook for 6–8 minutes, turning once, until crisp and golden. Arrange each burger on a bed of lettuce leaves, top with a spoonful of the mayonnaise, and serve immediately.

*LEFT: This design of cup could be found in many burger restaurants and diners earlier in the century.*

# Vancouver Venison Burgers
## with Crispy Potato Cakes

*Venison makes a delicious burger, but since the meat is very lean, it needs a little extra fat to keep it moist. Use unsmoked bacon, or pork fat if you can find it. Using the matzo meal or cornmeal in the potato cakes make them a little more crispy.*

1 tablespoon olive oil

1 onion, finely chopped

1 1/2 pounds venison shoulder or leg, trimmed and cut into small pieces

4 ounces bacon or pork fat

Salt and freshly ground black pepper

6–8 juniper berries, crushed

2–3 tablespoons vegetable oil

Lingonberry or cranberry sauce, to serve

### Crispy Potato Cakes

1 egg

Salt and freshly ground black pepper

1 small onion

2 small potatoes, peeled

1 tablespoon matzo meal or cornmeal (optional)

Vegetable oil for frying

1. Prepare the potato cakes. In a bowl, beat the egg and season with salt and pepper. Grate the onion and potato into a clean dish cloth and squeeze out as much of the liquid as possible. Transfer to the bowl with the egg and mix well. Stir in the matzo or cornmeal, if using.

2. Heat about 1 1/2 inch of oil in a heavy-based skillet over a medium–high heat. When very hot, drop 4 large spoonfuls of the potato mixture into the oil and flatten them slightly with a spatula. Cook for 3–5 minutes on each side, until crisp. Remove from the heat, drain on paper towels, and keep warm.

3. Heat the olive oil in a heavy-based skillet over a medium heat. Add the onions and cook for 3–4 minutes, until softened. Transfer to a bowl and let cool.

4. Put the venison and bacon or pork fat in the bowl of a food processor and process until finely chopped. Transfer to the bowl with the onions, season with the salt and pepper, and add the juniper berries. Using a fork, mix lightly until well combined. Shape into 4 patties, cover, and refrigerate.

5. Prepare an outdoor grill, or preheat an oven broiler. Arrange the patties on an oiled rack, or on a greased foil-lined broiler pan. Cook for 6–7 minutes, or longer for more well-done burgers, turning once. Arrange the potato cakes on 4 plates. Top each with a burger and a spoonful of the lingonberry or cranberry sauce.

# Oriental-Style Duck Burgers

## with Cucumber and Scallion

*Burgers made of duck meat are particularly well suited to grilling, which adds a slightly smoky flavor to the burger. Blinis or oriental pancakes, are available from specialist food stores; however, you may like to substitute another bread, such as pita.*

| | |
|---|---|
| 1 pound 10 ounces boneless, skinless, duck breast meat, cut into small pieces | 2 tablespoons Japanese soy sauce |
| 2–3 tablespoons bottled hoisin sauce | 1/2 teaspoon five-spice powder |
| 1–2 garlic cloves, finely chopped | Cayenne pepper |
| 2 scallions, finely chopped | 4 ready-made blinis or oriental pancakes |
| | Julienne of cucumber and scallion, to garnish |
| | Extra hoisin sauce, to serve |

1. Put the duck pieces in the bowl of a food processor and process until coarsely chopped. Transfer to a mixing bowl and add the hoisin sauce, garlic, scallions, soy sauce, five-spice powder, and cayenne pepper. Gently mix until well combined. Shape into 4 patties, cover, and refrigerate for 1 hour, or overnight.

2. Preheat the oven to 375°F. Arrange the blinis or oriental pancakes on a baking sheet and cover with foil. Bake for about 10 minutes, until heated through.

3. Prepare an outdoor charcoal, gas, or electric grill, or preheat an oven broiler. Arrange the patties on an oiled rack, or on a greased foil-lined broiler pan. Cook for 6–8 minutes, or longer for more well-done burgers, turning once. Alternatively, pan-fry in 2 tablespoons of vegetable oil for the same length of time.

*ABOVE: The perfect table ornament for burger addicts!*

4. Arrange the warm blinis or pancakes on a plate and spread each with a little hoisin sauce. Top each with a burger and a little extra hoisin sauce. Garnish with the cucumber and scallion, and serve immediately.

# Favorite Bacon-Cheese Burgers

*ABOVE: A tastefully designed cheeseburger radio, made by Amico in 1976.*

*This classic burger is an all-time favorite. You may like to serve it with Perfect Fries or Ski-Pole Fries, see page 91.*

8 slices bacon,
   cut in half

1³/₄ pounds ground beef
   (80% lean)

Salt and freshly ground
   black pepper

4 slices cheddar, Gruyére, or
   Monteray Jack cheese

4 burger buns, split and
   lightly toasted

Lettuce leaves

Sliced onion

Ketchup or other favorite
   condiments

1. Put the bacon slices in a large heavy-based skillet and place over a medium–high heat. Cook for 5–8 minutes, until the bacon is crisp and golden, turning once. Remove the bacon from the heat, drain on paper towels, and set aside.

2. Prepare an outdoor charcoal, gas, or electric grill, or preheat an oven broiler. Put the beef in a bowl and season with salt and pepper. Toss lightly and shape into 4 patties. Arrange the patties on an oiled rack, or a greased foil-lined broiler pan. Cook for 6–8 minutes, or longer for more well-done burgers, turning once. Top each burger with a slice of cheese 1 minute before the end of cooking, and let the cheese soften.

3. Arrange the lettuce on the bun bottoms and top each with a burger, 2 slices of bacon, some sliced onion, and ketchup or your favorite condiments. Serve immediately.

# Trattoria Burgers

## on Rosemary Focaccia

*Traditional Italian herbs and ingredients, such as oregano, radicchio, and arugula, are combined in this spicy burger. Use an aged provolone cheese for extra flavor.*

5–6 tablespoons extra-virgin olive oil

1 onion, chopped

2 cloves garlic, chopped

1 teaspoon dried oregano

1/2 teaspoon chopped fresh rosemary

1 pound ground beef (90% lean)

8 ounces ground pork

2 ounces pecorino romano or Parmesan cheese, grated

1 egg, beaten

1 tablespoon chopped fresh parsley

1 tablespoon chopped fresh basil

Salt and freshly ground black pepper

4 slices provolone cheese

Handful each of radicchio leaves, arugula, and watercress

1 tablespoon balsamic vinegar

4 slices rosemary focaccia bread, lightly toasted

Fresh rosemary sprigs, to garnish

1. Heat 1 tablespoon of the olive oil in a skillet. Add the onions and cook for 2–3 minutes, until softened and beginning to color. Add the garlic and herbs, and cook for 1–2 minutes more. Remove from the heat and set aside to cool.

2. Crumble the beef and pork into a large bowl and add the pecorino romano or Parmesan cheese. Toss lightly to combine. Add the egg, parsley, basil, and cooled onion mixture, and season with salt and pepper. Mix to combine well and shape into 4 burgers.

3. Heat 2 tablespoons of the oil in a large heavy-based skillet over a medium–hot heat. Add the patties and cook for 6–8 minutes, or slightly longer for more well-done burgers, turning once. Two minutes before the end of cooking, place one provolone slice on each burger to soften.

4. Put the radicchio, arugula, and watercress in a bowl, and toss with 2 tablespoons of olive oil and the balsamic vinegar. Season with salt and pepper. Brush the focaccia with a little oil and arrange on 4 plates. Top each focaccia slice a few dressed salad leaves and a burger. Garnish with rosemary and serve immediately.

*LEFT: A neon sign from Hot Cake House, Portland, Oregon.*

# ACCOMPANIMENTS

Classic accompaniments are essential for burgers. The variety of ketchups, burger relishes, barbecue sauces, and even salsas available in the average supermarket is staggering. However, it is fun to try your hand at a favorite – and it is certainly worth making your own french fries!

Use your imagination when selecting bread for your burgers. The classic soft bun, sometimes covered in sesame seeds, is always delicious, especially lightly toasted, but try different breads too, such as walnut and raisin or sun-dried tomato. Look for ethnic breads to use with burgers with a foreign flavor; pitas, naan bread, focaccia, and even bagels make great choices.

# Homemade Tomato Ketchup

4¹/₂ pounds very ripe, full-flavored tomatoes, chopped

4 onions, finely chopped

2 cloves garlic, chopped

1 tablespoon salt

1 tablespoon freshly ground black pepper

¹/₂ teaspoon cayenne pepper, or to taste

6 whole cloves

2 cups packed brown sugar

2 cups white wine vinegar

1. Place the tomatoes, onion, garlic, salt, pepper, cayenne pepper, and cloves in a large heavy-based saucepan over a medium heat. Simmer for about 45 minutes, until tender and juicy.

2. Reduce the heat to low, add the sugar and vinegar, and continue cooking until the sauce thickens, stirring frequently to prevent sticking.

3. Remove from the heat and strain the mixture through a strainer into a large bowl, pressing to extract all the sauce. Discard the tomato skins and any residue left in the strainer.

4. Ladle or pour the tomato ketchup into warm sterilized jars, and seal tightly with close-fitting lids. Label and store in a cool, dry place for at least 1 week before using.

*CLOCKWISE FROM LEFT: Homemade Tomato Ketchup; Tartar Sauce; Creamy Vinaigrette; Spicy Hamburger Relish.*

# Tartar Sauce

1/2 cup mayonnaise

3 tablespoons finely chopped
  dill pickles

1 tablespoon finely chopped
  onion

1 tablespoon chopped
  fresh parsley

2 teaspoons milk

1 teaspoon Dijon mustard

1. Combine all the ingredients in a small bowl, mixing until well blended. Cover with plastic wrap and refrigerate until ready to serve.

# Creamy Vinaigrette

1/4 cup white or
  red wine vinegar

1 tablespoon Dijon mustard

1/2 teaspoon salt

1 teaspoon sugar or honey
  (optional)

Freshly ground black pepper

3/4 cup olive or
  vegetable oil

1. Whisk the vinegar with the mustard, salt, and sugar or honey, if using, and season with pepper. Gradually add in the oil, whisking constantly until the vinaigrette is thick and creamy. Use immediately to dress salads, potatoes, or chilled, cooked vegetables.

# Spicy Hamburger Relish

5 large ripe beefsteak
  tomatoes, skinned,
  deseeded, and chopped

2 medium red onions, finely
  chopped

1 fresh green or red chili,
  finely chopped

2–3 cloves garlic, finely
  chopped

1-inch piece fresh ginger,
  peeled and finely
  chopped

1/2 cup red wine vinegar

1/2 cup light brown sugar,
  firmly packed

4 tablespoons tomato purée

1 teaspoon salt

1/2 teaspoon ground
  cinnamon

1/2 teaspoon ground cloves

1/2 teaspoon ground nutmeg

3/4 cup golden syrup

2 tablespoons chopped fresh
  mint or cilantro

1. Put all the ingredients, except the golden syrup and mint or cilantro, in a large stainless steel saucepan and bring to a boil over a medium–high heat. Reduce the heat to low and simmer, stirring occasionally, for about 1 hour, until the sauce is thickened.

2. Stir in the golden syrup and cook for 5 minutes more, stirring frequently. Remove from the heat and let cool to room temperature. Stir in the mint or cilantro, cover, and use as required. The relish will keep in the refrigerator for up to 2 weeks.

## Mayonnaise

2 egg yolks

2 tablespoons lemon juice
or white wine vinegar

1 tablespoon Dijon mustard

³/₄ teaspoon salt

¹/₄ teaspoon cayenne or
white pepper

1 cup olive or
vegetable oil, or half
olive and half
vegetable oil

1-2 tablespoons boiling
water (optional)

1. Using an electric mixer or whisk, beat the egg yolks, lemon juice or vinegar, mustard, salt, and cayenne or white pepper together until well blended. On medium speed, begin adding the oil, teaspoonful by teaspoonful. As it is incorporated, slowly pour in the oil in a very slow, thin stream, beating constantly until the mixture becomes thick, smooth, and emulsified.

2. Slowly beat in the boiling water and continue beating until cool. (Adding the boiling water will help extend the storage time, but it can be omitted.) Transfer the mayonnaise to a bowl, cover, and refrigerate for up to 3 days.

*CLOCKWISE FROM LEFT: Mayonnaise; Tomato, Onion, and Olive Relish; Easy Barbecue Sauce; "New Green" Pickles.*

## Tomato, Onion, and Olive Relish

1 tablespoon olive oil

1 large onion, coarsely
chopped

3 cloves garlic, finely
chopped

2 tablespoons balsamic or
cider vinegar

1 tablespoon sugar

¹/₂ teaspoon salt

Freshly ground black pepper

6 plum tomatoes, cored,
deseeded, and chopped

2 tablespoons chopped,
pitted, brine-cured
black olives

2 tablespoons chopped fresh
parsley or basil

1. Heat the oil in a medium-size saucepan over a medium heat. Add the onions and cook for 4–5 minutes, until softened. Add the garlic and cook for 1 minute more. Add the vinegar, sugar, salt, and pepper, and cook for 2 minutes more.

2. Add the tomatoes and toss to warm through, about 1 minute. Stir in the olives and chopped parsley or basil. Cook for 1 minute more. Remove from the heat, pour into a bowl, and let cool. Serve at room temperature.

# Easy Barbecue Sauce

2 tablespoons vegetable oil

1 small onion, finely chopped

2–3 cloves garlic, crushed

6–8 whole cloves

1/2 teaspoon cayenne pepper, or to taste

1/2 teaspoon cumin or cinnamon

1 cup Homemade Tomato Ketchup, see page 86, or a commercial variety

1/2 cup cider or malt vinegar

1/2 cup soy sauce

1/3 packed dark brown sugar

2 tablespoons Worcestershire sauce

1 tablespoon molasses (optional)

1. Heat the oil in a medium-size saucepan over a medium heat. Add the onion and cook for 3–4 minutes, until softened. Stir in the garlic, cloves, cayenne pepper, and cumin or cinnamon. Cook for 1–2 minutes more.

2. Add the remaining ingredients and simmer over a medium–low heat, stirring frequently, for about 20 minutes until the sauce is thickened.

3. Remove the pan from the heat and, if desired, strain through a strainer into a large bowl. Let cool, then cover and refrigerate until required.

# "New Green" Pickles

6 pickling cucumbers (Kirby or other small cucumbers)

5–6 large sprigs of dill

1/3 cup white wine vinegar

2 cups cold water

1 tablespoon salt

1 tablespoon sugar

12 black peppercorns, lightly crushed

1 teaspoon mustard seed, lightly crushed

2–3 cloves garlic, thickly sliced.

1. Cut each cucumber into 6 spears. Arrange them in a large, sealable pickling jar or other container. Insert the sprigs of dill into the jar.

2. Combine the vinegar, water, salt, sugar, peppercorns, mustard seed, and garlic in a large measuring pitcher. Stir to dissolve the sugar and salt, and pour the liquid over the cucumbers, making sure that they are completely covered. Close with a tight-fitting lid and refrigerate for at least 2 days before eating. The cucumbers will be slightly softened, but with a crisp, green look.

# Sautéed Potatoes

*For a slight variation, you can cook these potatoes from raw. Simply cut the potatoes into 1/2 inch dice and fry in hot oil, as described in the recipe. They will take slightly longer to cook.*

| | |
|---|---|
| 4 large potatoes | 1 onion, chopped (optional) |
| Vegetable oil for frying | Salt |

1. Put the potatoes in a large saucepan and cover with cold water. Bring to a boil over a medium–high heat and simmer for about 10 minutes, until just tender or slightly undercooked when pierced with the tip of a knife. Drain and rinse under cold running water to cool quickly. When cool, peel and cut into 1-inch cubes, or smaller.

2. Pour about 1/2 inch of oil into a large heavy-based skillet or wok and heat over a high heat, until very hot but not smoking.

3. Add the potatoes in a single layer, and cook for 3–4 minutes until golden brown. Using a slotted spoon or pancake turner, turn the potatoes and cook for 4–5 minutes more, turning as necessary to brown them evenly all over. If you like, add the onions 2–3 minutes before the end of the cooking time.

4. Remove the potatoes from the heat, drain well on paper towels, and sprinkle with salt to taste. Serve immediately, or keep warm in a moderate oven for up to 30 minutes.

*LEFT: Hart's Drive-In, Sacramento, California, in the '50s.*

*ABOVE: The Short Stop, Belleville, New Jersey.*

*BELOW, FROM LEFT: Ski-Pole Fries; Sautéed Potatoes; Perfect Fries.*

# Perfect Fries

*When deep-frying the potatoes, make sure you do not add too many at once, or else the temperature of the oil will drop. It is best to work in manageable batches, keeping the cooked french fries warm in the oven while you are cooking the rest.*

**5–6 large potatoes**　　**Vegetable oil for**
**Salt**　　　　　　　　　　**frying**

1. Trim each potato into a square-sided shape. Cut lengthwise into 1/2-inch slices, then stack and cut the slices into 1/2-inch sticks. Rinse the cut potatoes in cold water and dry well in a clean dish cloth or pat dry with paper towels.

2. Pour at least 3 inches of oil into a large, deep saucepan, or deep-fat fryer, and heat to 325°F, or until a cube of bread browns in 30 seconds. Fry the potatoes in batches for 5–6 minutes, until tender and just beginning to color. Remove with a slotted spoon and drain on paper towels.

*LEFT: Art-Deco-style Yum-Yum "burgerbars'" were located throughout the San Fernando valley, California.*

3. Just before serving, reheat the oil to the hotter temperature of 375°F, and refry the potatoes for 2–3 minutes, until crisp and golden. Remove and drain on paper towels. Sprinkle the fries with salt, and serve while hot.

# Ski-Pole Fries

Cut the potatoes into thin sticks, about 1/4-inch wide and as long as possible, leaving the ends pointed, rather than squared off. Deep-fry, following the method for the Perfect Fries, but for only one frying, at 375°F for 6–10 minutes, until crisp and golden.

*BELOW: A 1949 advert for "enriched bread and flour," published by the Wheat Flour Institute in 1949.*

# Index

**Acknowledgments**

The Publishers wish to thank the following collectors, organisations and picture libraries who have supplied the photographs (and/or items for photography) that are featured in the book: John Baeder; Lake County (IL) Museum, Curt Teich Postcard Archives; Richard J. S. Gutman; Jim Heimann; Larry Kantor; Bob Lange; Ruby Montana; White Castle System, Inc.; Harry Sperl; and Wendy's International.

**Picture credits**

Photographs have been credited by page number and position on the page: (B) Bottom, (T) Top, (C) Center, (BL) Bottom left, etc. The names of contributing organisations, collectors and libraries have been abbreviated as follows: John Baeder (JB); Lake County (IL) Museum, Curt Teich Postcard Archives (CT); Richard J. S. Gutman (RG); Jim Heimann (JH); Larry Kantor (LK); Bob Lange (BL); Ruby Montana (RM); White Castle System, Inc. (WCS); Harry Sperl (HS).

5: RG; 6: JH; 8: LK (T); WCS/HS (B); 9: JH (CL); CT (BL); HS (TR, CR); 10: RG (BL); JH (TR); 11: RG (CL); HS (TR, B); 12: LK; 13: JH (L, R); 14/15: CT; 16: RG; 18: HS; 19: RM; 20: RG; 21: JH; 22: BL; 23: HS; 24: HS; 26/27: RG; 28: JH (BL); LK (TR); 30: JB; 31: HS (T, B); 33: CT; 34: RG; 35: RG; 36: HS; 38/39: RG; 40: HS; 42: Wendy's International, photo by Neal Lauron; 44: HS; 45: RG (T); 46: JH; 47: JH; 48: WCS (T, B); 50/51: JH; 52: JH; 54: CT; 56: CT; 57: JH; 58: JH (L, R); 59: HS; 60: CT; 62/63: JH; 64: JH; 66: HS; 67: JH; 68: JH; 69: HS; 70: JH (TL); CT (TR); 71: RG (T); HS (B); 72: JH; 74/75: RG; 76: RM; 78: RM; 80: HS; 81: HS; 82: RG; 86: HS; 87: JH; 88: HS; 89: JH; 90: JH (BL); RG (TR); 91: JH (L); HS (R); 93: HS; Front and back endpapers: RG; Back cover: JH (TL); HS (CR); Wendy's International/Neal Lauron (BR).